New Communities for Urban Squatters

Lessons from the Plan That Failed in
Dhaka, Bangladesh

Urban Innovation Abroad

Series Editor: Thomas L. Blair
The Martin Center for Architectural and Urban Studies,
University of Cambridge, Cambridge, England

Urbanization, despite its many severe consequences, has given a healthy stimulus to urban innovation in developing countries. This series seeks to share with an international readership the ideas and experiences of policy-makers, planners, academics, and researchers actively engaged in the day-to-day planning, design, and management of Third World cities.

NEW COMMUNITIES FOR URBAN SQUATTERS: Lessons from the Plan That Failed in Dhaka, Bangladesh
    Charles L. Choguill

STRENGTHENING URBAN MANAGEMENT: International Perspectives and Issues
    Edited by Thomas L. Blair

URBAN INNOVATION ABROAD
Problem Cities in Search of Solutions
    Edited by Thomas L. Blair

A Continuation Order Plan is available for this series. A continuation order will bring delivery of each new volume immediately upon publication. Volumes are billed only upon actual shipment. For further information please contact the publisher.

New Communities for Urban Squatters

Lessons from the Plan That Failed in Dhaka, Bangladesh

Charles L. Choguill
University of Sheffield
Sheffield, England

PLENUM PRESS • NEW YORK AND LONDON

Library of Congress Cataloging in Publication Data

Choguill, Charles L.
  New communities for urban squatters.

  (Urban innovation abroad)
  Bibliography: p.
  Includes index.
  1. Squatter settlements—Bangladesh—Dhaka. 2. Urban policy—Bangladesh—
Dhaka. 3. Housing policy—Bangladesh—Dhaka. 4. City planning—Bangladesh—
Dhaka. I. Title. II. Series.
HD7361.6.D57C36   1987   307.3′36   86-30501
ISBN 0-306-42545-9

C

© 1987 Plenum Press, New York
A Division of Plenum Publishing Corporation
233 Spring Street, New York, N.Y. 10013

Printed in the United States of America

Preface

This is a book on the interrelatedness of planning and implementation, on how policymakers and planners can be more effective in solving problems of providing new homes and settlements for urban squatters in developing countries. It treats a subject which in this year of publication, The United Nations International Year of Shelter for the Homeless, has attracted global interest and concern.

New Communities for Urban Squatters helps us to understand the ways in which the planning process is being redefined as it moves into the mainstream of urban change and political decisionmaking. Resettlement of squatters in new urban communities is one option open to planners to meet the housing and settlement needs of low-income residents of Third World cities. In too many cases, however, the plans have failed to achieve their objectives for reasons which could have been foreseen and dealt with at the outset.

For resettlement and new community building to be a feasible solution, this book argues, plan implementation as well as plan preparation must be considered as basic and inseparable parts of the planning process. Success depends on getting right the five fundamental aspects of planning which have Third World-wide significance: appropriate organizational structures and coordination, finance, technology, cultural understanding, and public participation. If not, failure is sure to follow.

The author, Charles L. Choguill brings to this authoritative work a broad background in consulting, planning, and teaching. He is Reader in Development Planning in the Department of Town and Regional Planning, University of Sheffield, England, and holds a Ph.D in Regional Science from the University of Pennsylvania. He has observed and worked in Bangladesh and other developing nations on behalf of the United Nations Development Program and the Asian Development Bank.

To illustrate his arguments Choguill examines a new community project at Mirpur for squatters decanted from Dhaka, capital of Bangladesh - from its conception to its final abandonment. Historical, political and demographic pressures accelerating urbanization and squatting are discussed. The role of central government and municipal agencies, United Nations and international non-governmental organizations are assessed. Settlement planning policies and strategies and project documents are given detailed attention, as are financial issues of affordability, cost recovery, and project replicability.

The author concludes with concrete proposals for modifying planning theory, practice and policy. Recommendations are directed to policymakers and planners at the domestic and international levels.

The book will be of practical use to professional and academic urban planners, architects, engineers, project management and financial analysts, and to consultants and officials of international organizations and governments concerned with urban planning and implementation in Third World cities. Students in both the developed and developing countries will find the book of great value because of its systematic overview of one entire project and its portrayal of lessons which can be learned from a plan that failed.

New Communities for Urban Squatters takes its place in the Urban Innovation Abroad series as a detailed case study and state-of-the-art survey. It is an essential companion volume to Strengthening Urban Management which covers a wide range of problems and approaches to the provision of housing, transportation, finance, and manpower in contrasting urban situations. In spirit, Choguill's work also reflects the positive goals expressed in a related Plenum publication, Urban Innovation Abroad: Problem Cities in Search of Solutions, which places planning in the setting of the international effort for equitable development and the effective improvement of human settlements.

We are grateful for the enthusiasm and skill which Charles Choguill has brought to writing this book.

Thomas L. Blair, Series Editor
Urban Innovation Abroad

Note

In 1983, the Government of Bangladesh officially changed the English spelling of their capital city from Dacca to Dhaka, suggesting that phonetically the latter spelling was closer to that of the Bengali language than the former. The new spelling has been adopted throughout even for references to the city prior to 1983 except where Dacca is used in direct quotation or the title of a book or article published prior to that date. Even in these cases, place of publication is given with the new spelling.

Contents

Figures

Tables

1. The Importance of Implementation

Implementation is one of the most crucial aspects of any planning exercise. Plans which do not result in tangible change represent little more than a waste of planning resources. Within the development context, where resources of all types are generally scarce, successful implementation is the most critical of all issues in the process of planning growth and development.

Unfortunately, experience reveals that implementation is one of the most problematic elements of the planning process. Regardless of whether one is examining the planning process at the macro-level of national economic plans, or at the micro-level of local land-use plans, one set of planning skills seems more readily available than another. As one national plan observes (Republic of Nigeria, 1970, p. 333), "Implementing a plan is as important as, if not more important than, drawing up the plan. Experience has shown that even with the best planning techniques, there is usually a gap between plan formulation and plan implementation". More to the point perhaps is the observation that the late Prime Minister Nehru (1961, p. 435) reportedly made concerning Indian experience, "... We are not quite so expert at implementation as at planning ..."

As a result of this discrepancy in skills, a survey of many Third World nations reveals a landscape littered with shattered hopes and dreams: unimplemented plans that collect dust in the archives and partially completed projects which might have been finished except for flaws in the implemen-

1

tation process which prevented them from meeting the need for which they were designed.

This book argues that both plan preparation and plan implementation are basic and inseparable parts of the planning process. It is further suggested that the majority of implementation problems that arise in the planning process in Third World nations are foreseeable and, as Waterston (1965, p. 314) has observed "... the lack of success in implementing plans is in large part attributable to poor planning"[1]. Of course there are always random events which constrain implementation but far too often they are merely an excuse for inadequate consideration of problems which should have been anticipated. If allowance is made in plan-making to compensate for known areas of weakness in plan implementation, i.e., the non-random factors, the probability of avoiding failure is greatly enhanced.

To illustrate these arguments, a detailed examination is made of the planning and implementation of a small squatter resettlement project that was attempted in Bangladesh. In January 1975, about 173,000 bastuharas (literally, "shelterless") were forcibly removed from Dhaka. The initial plans were to resettle the squatters at three camps, each a considerable distance from the center of the city. The plans for two of these resettlement sites, at Tongi and Demra, were implemented, although with difficulty. The third at Mirpur, provides the case study material for the present analysis, revealing a wide range of implementation problems that frequently arise when new communities are designed and built in a resource-scarce situation.

As a result of this clearance of the squatters from Dhaka, 3,044 families were deposited at Bashantek, within the municipality of Mirpur[2], on an unimproved and temporary site to the north of the capital city. Although plans were periodically suggested to provide a permanent home for the former squatters, it was not until intervention by United Nations personnel took place in March 1977 that a final site and project plan was devised. It is the various attempts to design and implement this plan between 1978 and 1981 that provide the empirical material of the present study and illustrate the chasm that can exist between planning and implementation with such disastrous results.

The project itself is broken up into component parts, each part encompassing a series of planning steps, or sets of decisions. The plans which resulted are examined in light of other information that was known at the time. The project itself was never finished. The reasons for this failure to complete the squatter resettlement project are of paramount interest in the present analysis. The fundamental question is that at the end of the day, how many of the implementation problems encountered by the project could have been identified before they occurred? Would this additional knowledge have allowed revision in the plan-making which might have led to the successful completion of the project? It is argued here that the answer to the second question is almost certainly in the affirmative.

IMPLEMENTATION WITHIN THE PLANNING PROCESS

The importance of the analysis of implementation is a relatively new area of concern within the planning field as until the early 1970s, the planning literature was more oriented to plan-making than to plan implementation. Among those concerned with planning in the Third World, the central role of implementation is an even more recent discovery (Vepa, 1974; reprinted in Rondinelli, 1977). In one sense, this is surprising, for this has long been one of the most serious impediments constraining the efforts of planners in developing countries.

Much of what planners think of the implementation process comes not from their own field but has been borrowed from the field of policy analysis (Barrett and Fudge, 1981, Chapter 1). In the late 1960s and early 1970s, American academics in the policy field became increasingly concerned about the implementation of US Federal Government programs in various parts of the country. Policies passed by the Congress seemed at times to emerge on the ground in quite a different form than one might have expected from reading the original legislation. In some states, the programs seemed to work better than in others. Furthermore, the implementation of certain kinds of policy seemed far more difficult than putting other elements of a program into operation.

In 1973, Pressman and Wildavsky published their now famous study of the implementation problems associated with the US Economic Development Administration (EDA) program in Oakland, California, concluding that "we have learned one important lesson from the EDA experience in Oakland: implementation should not be divorced from policy. There is no point in having good ideas if they cannot be carried out" (Pressman and Wildavsky, 1973, p. 143). Other policy analysts became concerned with this elusive link between good ideas and carrying them out and a theoretical basis for the consideration of such problems in the policy formulation process began to emerge[3].

By the mid-1970s, the implementation problem was under examination by urban and regional planners as well, beginning with early work by Friedmann (1972) and Faludi (1973, Chapter 15), both of whom suggested that successful implementation of plans was a function of effective power. This seemed perfectly consistent with the traditional view of the planning system which postulated decision-chains, with each step in the planning process following logically from the one before, leading to the characterization of this sequence as the rational decision model[4].

Yet one problem which emerges from such a formulation is that planning decisions are seen as passing almost automatically from one box to another through a flow diagram. The desirability of a particular change is expressed. Information is gathered. It is evaluated. A decision is made. It is implemented. Although feedback loops may well be incorporated from the bottom to the top of such schematic diagrams, the fact remains that implementation might well be viewed as quite a distinct process from that of planning and might even be carried out by distinct groups of people. For all practical purposes, the implementation of a plan might, under such conditions, be taking place on the far side of the moon.

Both Friedmann and Faludi have recognized this danger and argued strongly against such compartmentalization. Faludi, for example, suggests (1973, pp. 278-279) that implementation problems arise primarily because of the inadequacies in program formulation. Program formulation in turn can be faulty because of the imperfect knowledge planners have of the outside world or because of their misconception of the control that they exercise over the various actors in the implementation process. Improvement occurs largely through changes in both of these spheres, a process which would seem to necessitate a breaking down of this wall between planning and implementation. Friedmann (1967, p. 240) expresses the same argument even more concisely, as "the kind of implementation mechanism adopted will itself influence the character of the plan and the way it is formulated".

The theoretical foundations for the analysis of implementation quickly spread to planning practioners. In 1977, the Technical Co-operation Service of the Organization for Economic Co-operation and Development sponsored a Symposium on the Implementation of Urban Plans and planners from major cities shared their common problems. Among the more interesting presentations at the Symposium were those from planners in the OECD's poorer European "southern fringe" states, such as Greece, Turkey, Portugal and Yugoslavia (Costa Lobo, 1977; Dekleva, Bon and Music, 1977; Ataç, 1977; Aneroussi, 1977).

Not surprisingly, the issues of urban and regional planning implementation attracted attention as well in the developing world where by comparison the shortages of resources, lack of planning infrastructure, and difficulties of implementation were very much greater. Although some notable successes in the implementation of urban planning projects in the developing world have occurred, the number of instances of less than optimal implementation or actual project failures, is very high.

DEFINING FAILURE IN IMPLEMENTATION[5]

A "failure" is obviously something that does not succeed. Yet in planning, such a straightforward definition is somewhat harder to isolate. Buildings that may not be totally appropriate for some intended use may be transferred successfully to alternative uses. Transport projects, such as new roads, are notoriously difficult to identify as a failure due to the long life expected of them and to the perpetually increasing demand for their use.

The measurement of success becomes an even more complex matter when it is realized that the seriousness of a failure varies with the type of project under consideration. A bridge over a deep canyon that can be no more than 90% completed is an obvious failure, yet a housing program which provides no more than 90% of the expected units may not necessarily be considered a failure at all. A rail line between two major cities, linking intermediate stations, is not necessarily a failure if only 90% of its length can be constructed.

This seems to suggest that "failure" and "success" are not dichotomous, but merely represent end-points on a scale between them. Depending on the kind of project being implemented, the distance between the ends of this scale can be subjectively interpreted as tending toward success or failure. In the case of the bridge, 90% completion represented a failure because it was of no use, while in the housing project, it was nearer to being a success as it at least partially met the objectives set for the project.

The implementation of a planning project tends toward failure if it:

i   fails to achieve the realistic objectives of the planners because of the way that it was planned or carried out;
ii   leads to unexpected costs above and beyond an original reasonable allocation of resources (such as unexpected losses to national income, unexpected resource use or maintenance costs).

Even with these criteria, value-laden words creep in, such as "realistic objectives" and "reasonable allocation of resources". If the cost does not exceed the expected expenditure of the proposed project during implementation it may still tend to be a failure in planning terms if the funds could have been better applied in alternative uses. In such cases as these, the implementation process itself could have been a total success. Or alternatively, even an unsound plan could be implemented in a satisfactory manner, a situation that could readily result in a failure.

In the analysis in the following chapters, the squatter resettlement project at Mirpur is a failure in terms of the two criteria listed above. The project ended up far closer to one end of the continuum than to the middle. As a result, the steps which led to this conclusion are readily analyzed and, hopefully, lessons which might affect future projects can be learned.

DEFINING THE PLANNING PROCESS

Throughout this analysis, the relationship between the "planning process" and "implementation" forms a vital link. The "planning process" puts together plans and policies which are designed to result in specific and identifiable end products, such as improved housing within an area, or reduced transportation costs as a result of planned improvements within the transport network. The overall objective of the planning process then is to improve an "environment".

Particularly within the Third World context, but also to a somewhat lesser extent within developed countries as well, this improvement of the "environment" is accomplished by the planning and design of specific projects, that is by executing "positive powers". These powers contrast with the exercise of "negative powers" which might be associated with the development control aspects within an existing environment. A number of "contributors" are associated with each planning project, feeding various kinds of inputs such as materials, skills and finance into the project according to some relatively fixed schedule.

As there are a number of contributors to each major project, it is apparent that some kind of co-ordination is required. In all but those countries least prepared for planning and implementation, the "co-ordination of implementation" process and the "planning process" might be fused, as suggested by Friedmann and Faludi, with interactive links between them. Hopefully, the day when planners planned and engineers implemented is a thing of the past although for those familiar with planning in a number of Third World nations, such a hope is probably without foundation.

"Negative powers" are equally important to the planners, particularly within an urban environment, including such vital elements as the control of planned development, development control and the enforcement of statutory plans. One could argue that negative powers are more integrally a part of the planning process than of a separate implementation process. Yet such powers are very much a part of the implementation process itself for without them, much of the potential gain from planning activity would be lost.

The present study of squatter resettlement in Bangladesh is concerned with the positive planning powers as they relate to project planning. Redevelopment and renewal in Bangladesh are briefly considered but they are primarily included because they in turn affect the planning and implementation of urban planning projects rather than for their own merit.

CONSTRAINTS ON IMPLEMENTATION

The planning process does not, however, automatically result in successful implementation of planning projects. A number of constraints exist which unless adequately allowed for, are likely to result in projects which tend more toward failure than success. Five, distinctly identifiable, sets of implementation problems played a major role in the outcome of the Bangladesh squatter resettlement scheme. Each of these constraints, it is argued, was foreseeable and could conceivably have been explicitly considered in the planning process of the project, and hence probably have been avoided.

Organizational Issues

The first of these is concerned with organizational issues. This impediment to implementation seems to affect both the development control sphere and project planning and is often characterized by an inadequately co-ordinated and organized institutional framework. Within the development control area, such constraints can arise from numerous sources. Among Commonwealth nations, many have adopted legislation based upon the legal framework developed in the United Kingdom whether the objectives of such legislation are appropriate or not to local situations. In such cases, adaption of the British system of local administration may be adequate for dealing with day-to-day administration, but it copes poorly with the key problems associated with development, expansion of infrastructural facilities and the implementation of essential planning schemes.

In project planning exercises, these issues are particularly relevant, especially when either the planning or implementation process may be undertaken by different agencies, each with their own structure, goals and objectives. Projects may be seen in a different light by each participating organization resulting in conflict among differing objectives and sub-optimal implementation. Unless there can be some consensus on the project goals by the participating agencies, it is unlikely that fully successful implementation can be achieved.

Closely related, and therefore included here under organizational issues, is the problem of the amount of change involved in a project.   Van Meter and Van Horn (1975) have suggested that with respect to policy, small changes are far more likely to be achieved than large ones.   Within the sphere of project planning, a similar observation appears to have relevance.   Smaller projects are probably less complicated to complete than large projects, and so too are projects which require fewer rather than more contributors.

The location of organizations themselves can also be viewed as one element of this problem.   If the physical distance separating the "planning process" agencies and perhaps even the "co-ordinators of implementation" from the contributors to the project, or the people who are the recipients of the project, is great, then the monitoring process which is desirably associated with the project may be severely constrained.   This is, of course, part of the traditional problem of centralization versus decentralization in planning.

Lack of Resources

The second major reason for failure in implementation, and one which, like the first, can frequently have political overtones, is the problem of resource scarcity.   Lack of resources forms a primary threat to project planning exercises but is frequently found to have some effect upon development control activities as well.   In many developing nations, a common characteristic is a severe constraint upon the monetary resources available for allocation to planning projects.   Lack of such monetary resources is obviously one prime definition of under-development.   Yet as viewed here, lack of resources goes considerably further.   Trained planners and engineers may be in short supply leading to a situation where practitioners are necessarily forced to make decisions within fields where they have little knowledge. The results of such decisions, not withstanding the dedication of the personnel involved, can result in projects that could be better planned and implemented if the properly trained and experienced manpower resources had been available.

A similar situation exists with respect to land
resources. Where the demand from the population for food
exceeds supply, an obvious policy instrument that could be
applied is to preserve by some means agriculturally pro-
ductive land. The implication to the urban project planner
may be to build at high densities which in turn affects the
built form. As a result, architects who may recognize within
their country a traditional inheritance of single-storey
houses may receive terms of reference from political decision-
makers to build multi-storey flats. The imposition of such
alien structures upon traditional society can have a devas-
tating psychological and sociological effect which results
directly from responses to the resource shortage of land.

Alternatively, shortage of land resources can have
other effects upon project success. Squatter resettlement
projects are frequently relegated to peripheral locations
where urban land is cheaper even though such residents
traditionally find work most easily in the center of the city.
Or land which can be used for no other purposes, perhaps
because it is subject to flooding, might be allocated to
residential development as a means of saving agricultural
land. In either case, the cause is associated with a
shortage in the supply of a particular resource compared to
its demand, in this case, land.

Ironically, where resources are scarce, underspending
is an equally serious problem. Certainly a shortfall in the
expenditure of allocated funds for a project is an indication
of something wrong either in the way the plan was formulated or in its implementation (Waterston, 1965, p. 302).
Such deficiencies could reflect inappropriate administrative
structures, a lack of complementary resources, inadequate
phasing or simply deficiencies in plans and designs.

Cultural Understanding

A third factor which might be identified as a potentially
severe constraint upon the implementation process is lack of
cultural understanding. It is suggested that this factor can
adversely affect the project realization process in several
different ways. Foreign consultants, whether based with
commercial firms, international organizations or bilateral
aid-giving institutions, frequently find themselves not really
grasping the inherent problems of the host country. Even
consultants who make an effort to understand the local

reality may find themselves unable to translate their cultural awareness into objective plan components.

Yet the problem is not unique to expatriates. Even within the country itself, civil servants from educated, upper- and middle-income urban backgrounds, may have tremendous difficulty in grasping the true problems of the poor from agricultural areas. The cultural gap between different social groups even within a single country may be virtually too wide to bridge.

Cultural constraints can, however, take other forms that may be equally damaging. Lipton (1977) argues that the entire national planning process, and in fact, the entire way we look at the development question, is biased towards urban areas[6].

One might also note that even within a nation's urban structure, there is an inherent bias toward investing in capital cities. This takes place because national decision makers are normally urban residents and are, in fact, usually residents of the national capital. Not only are decision-makers improving their own environment by approving proposals for better infrastructure for the capital city but they are also attempting to find possible solutions to problems they see most frequently. Yet the result of such continued and disproportionate investments in urban areas means that cities grow. This growth represents one of the many 'vicious circles' which affect Third World cities. Improvement in infrastructure (transport, electricity, water, drains) enhances the large urban area's industrial location advantage compared to other areas. Firms wishing to minimize their costs of production choose these areas for new investment. New investment in turn leads to greater employment opportunity, creating economic disparities within the nation. Such employment opportunities result in accelerated rural-to-urban migration since most migration is based on the prospect of better jobs and hence higher incomes. With greater urban populations, the need arises for still further improvements and extensions of the infrastructural network.

Inappropriate Technology

The fourth factor which might be expected to adversely affect implementation is technology. Like other problems, this takes several forms. One is the overuse of advanced technologies. All too frequently in the developing world, the entire development process is thought of as to modernize or to Westernize. This is seen as the harnessing and utilization of high technology regardless of whether there is a tradition of such innovation in the country. Hence it is not surprising to find examples of urban project planners using high technology solutions to solve traditional problems whether they are appropriate or not. Examples include mass transit solutions (such as metro systems) to solve circulation problems, high-rise (frequently industrially-produced) housing to solve accommodation shortages and the incorporation of high and possibly inappropriate usage standards in the provision of water[7].

The use of inappropriate technology also creates problems for a nation's construction industry. Whereas construction companies in Third World countries may cope remarkably well with traditional building styles, when confronted with imported designs, complex problems arise in terms of specifications, adapting local materials to new uses, learning new techniques and establishing new procedures of quality control and supervision. Leaky roofs, gaping joints and poor finishes may be the result. Many of the lessons of the current case study are concerned with these very issues[8].

In turn, construction difficulties frequently result in a failure to meet timetables and construction schedules. The cost of such delays is higher than any developing country can afford. If later elements of a project are delayed due to time extensions of earlier parts because of difficulties resulting from the technical matters in building construction, a rise in costs is inevitable.

Inadequate Public Participation

The fifth of these constraints is concerned with the all-too-frequent exclusion of the target population from the planning and implementation process. Almost all urban planning activity is concerned with improving the lives of the urban population. This is true whether such activity is concerned with neighborhood up-grading schemes, transportation projects, market developments or inner city improvements. Plans which incorporate no more than the ideas of the planners are likely to be disappointing to that public for which they were intended. Thus, in recent years, some planners have turned to formal and informal discussions with target groups to insure that a broader range of ideas are incorporated into the planning stage of such projects. Although the plan devised in such a manner may not even be all that different from one which the planners may have devised in isolation, the results are far more likely to be generally accepted by all parties affected by such schemes.

It is apparent that public participation in the planning stages of a planning project can take many forms. Some years ago, Arnstein (1969) devised a ladder of citizen participation. These levels of involvement ranged from "non-participation", including "manipulation" and "therapy", through "degrees of tokenism", comprised of "informing", "consultation" and "placation", to "degrees of citizen power", such as "delegated power" and the highest level of involvement, "citizen control". Such a scheme would seem to have value in determining the type of participation that was most appropriate to any given planning exercise. At the same time, the ladder reveals how quickly true participation of the public in such an exercise drops off into degrees of tokenism.

The incorporation of the public into a planning exercise would seem to be as important to implementation as it is in the planning process. If a scheme has broadly-based public support, politicians are far less likely to lose interest in it if problems develop. As enthusiasm is contagious, planners are likely to devote extra effort to schemes when they have popular public support.

METHODOLOGICAL ISSUES

These five categories of implementation problems will be examined later in far greater detail with the aid of the case study of the Mirpur Resettlement Project which facilitates the in-depth reconstruction of a series of complex and inter-related effects. It is recognized that reservations might be expressed concerning the generality of the conclusions which can be extracted from the narrative or the validity of the conclusions which can be reached from a single study in terms of the five very broad sets of implementation constraints considered here. Yet it would seem that the kinds

of problems encountered in implementing the Mirpur Resettlement Project are representative of those encountered in other
projects in the field of urban development. As Mirpur
comprised a fairly complex undertaking, it was likely that a
wide range of difficulties would emerge and this in turn may
have made the implementation process itself more complex.
The emphasis in this work is, however, not so much concerned with achieving perfect generality, but in attempting
to see if problems encountered at Mirpur could have been
foreseen and steps taken to circumvent the difficulties that
might therefore have been expected.

Whereas the present chapter establishes the importance
of implementation in the planning process and the kinds of
problems which are likely to arise when it is carried out,
later chapters are directed specifically to the Bangladesh
situation and the implementation process of the Mirpur
project.

Chapter 2 considers the recent urban development of
Bangladesh and the likely effects of rapid urbanization.
Special emphasis is directed toward the capital city, Dhaka.
Here, as elsewhere in the world, rapid increases in population led to unauthorized housing in various parts of the
city. Dhaka's methods of coping with its increasing number
of new residents, particularly the squatters in unauthorized
settlements, as well as their characteristics, are examined.

Chapter 3 is devoted to the various approaches to the
housing problem followed by past governments, starting with
the early policies and programs followed by Pakistan.
Equally important is the identification of the factors which
have historically affected this policy as they might well be
expected to have some impact on any housing related
project. These factors include the urban planning system in
Bangladesh, financial constraints and the structure of
Bangladesh society. The nation's increasing reliance upon
outside agencies for assistance in the housing field is also
examined.

Chapter 4 focuses on national government attitudes
toward squatters which had a profound effect upon project
planning and were a factor in the decision to remove
squatters from the streets of Dhaka and relocate them in
peripheral locations. The early events in the removal

process are noted, and the later important role played by international voluntary organizations is discussed.

With Chapter 5, the level of analysis shifts from the general to the increasingly specific. The actual planning of the Mirpur Resettlement Project is considered, as well as the evolution of the project's design, the solutions suggested for specific problems, and an evaluation of the organizational element of project planning and implementation.

The important issue of financial feasibility provides the subject matter of Chapter 6. The chapter first tries to determine whether or not the project as planned was capable of meeting the financial objectives set by the Government of Bangladesh, and then considers various alternative means of reducing construction costs as a way of improving the economic aspects of the resettlement scheme.

Chapter 7 focuses on the plans which were made for project implementation and the results of these efforts. Three elements play a central role in this consideration: the attempt to achieve a co-ordinated effort in the implementation process, the state of the Bangladesh construction industry, and the monitoring procedures which were established.

The concluding Chapter 8 restates the arguments which have been developed and considers their applicability to the problems and experiences of other Third World nations.

ACKNOWLEDGEMENTS

The book is the product of a long-standing experience with the urban and regional development problems of Bangladesh. From 1974 to 1979, the University of Sheffield was involved in a United Nations sponsored Joint Masters Degree program in Urban and Regional Planning with the Bangladesh University of Engineering and Technology. During this time frequent trips were made to Bangladesh to review a variety of urban development efforts undertaken by the fledgling government of the new nation, one of these was the Mirpur Squatter Resettlement Project.

In preparing this book, I have received considerable encouragement from many people. At the very earliest stages of the research in 1980, Bruce Mecartney, Director of the United Nations Development Program project on Bangladesh Housing Policies and Programs opened his files on the project and discussed them at great length. His death the following year was a loss both personally and to Third World urban development.

Very significant assistance was given by Government officials in Bangladesh, to whom I am greatly indebted for their interest and unflagging support.

Cesar Solis, Director of the United Nations Development Program Bangladesh National Physical Planning Project introduced me to many of the project participants. Golam Rahman of the Bangladesh University of Engineering and Technology directed me to relevant research. Nazrul Islam of Dhaka University's Center for Urban Studies provided survey material that appears in the study. Moinrul Islam, who was Permanent Secretary of the Bangladesh Ministry of Public Works at the time the project was conceived, gave a first-hand account of planning at its earliest stages. David Campbell, OXFAM representative to Bangladesh, and Sheena Grossett from OXFAM headquarters, provided information on the contributions of non-government organizations to the project. A number of my own past students have carried out research in allied areas and their names appear frequently in footnotes to the analysis. These include Tanvir Khan, Rob Gallagher, Tasleem Shakur, Md. Ahmeduzzaman and Md. Khorshed Alam.

Finally, I owe a special debt to Thomas L. Blair, editor of the Urban Innovation Abroad series, who made constructive suggestions at numerous points along the way. Gillian Teet prepared the diagrams and helped with much of the typing, assisted by Chris Homes, Jane Allonby and Jeanette Leaman.

My wife, Kathryn-Anne, deserves a special personal note of thanks as she tolerated my sometimes lengthy trips to Bangladesh and the trauma of analysis and writing. It is to her that this book is dedicated.

Conceptual errors are mine alone.

Charles L. Choguill
University of Sheffield, UK
July 1986

2. The Accelerating Urbanization of Bangladesh

Bangladesh, with an estimated present population of something in excess of 100 million crammed into an area of no more than 55,000 square miles, has one of the highest population densities in the world, surpassed only by Hong Kong, Singapore and Malta. In fact, if the entire population of the world were placed in Australia, the density per square mile would approximately equal that of Bangladesh.

Bangladesh is also one of the world's least urbanized nations. According to the census of 1981, 15% of the population lived in urban areas defined as having at least 5,000 residents (Bangladesh Bureau of Statistics, 1983, Chapter 3). The rural areas can be characterized as areas of low productivity, high rates of population increase and a high man-to-land ratio.

Over the last two decades, change has begun to occur in Bangladesh as more and more rural residents migrate to urban areas. Rates of urbanization grew from 5% in 1961 to almost 9% in 1974[1]. During this period, the number of urban squatters in the major cities of Bangladesh increased rapidly. These squatters, and the events which befell them, form a central focus of concern of this book.

Squatting is the result of a number of interrelated forces. These factors include rural poverty, rural-to-urban migration, excess demand for reasonably priced housing, lack of urban economic opportunity, war, natural disasters and failure of government development policies. Each of these factors has played a role within the Bangladesh (and

17

previously the East Pakistan) environment although obviously, as in most countries, some of these factors have been more important than others. At the same time, as we will see, certain Bangladesh cities have been less successful in coping with the new migrants than they were in attracting them.

This migration, and the rapid urbanization which resulted, as shown in Table 1 for the largest cities in the nation, is viewed here as the first of a series of major constraints upon the eventual implementation of the Mirpur project. Because of the increases in urban population and the limited urban economic opportunities that these migrants encountered upon their arrival in the cities such as Dhaka, Khulna and Chittagong, squatting, i.e., the unauthorized use of urban land, became the only alternative open to them in finding a place to live. As a result, pressures were put on the planners to find a solution to what many considered to be a problem, and ill-considered policies were adopted and implemented.

MIGRATION FROM THE RURAL AREAS

Rapid urban growth in Bangladesh cities is the result of both rural "push" factors and urban "pull" factors. At times, in recent years, these factors have affected rural residents' decisions to migrate with varying intensities. Although rural push factors have probably been more important than the lure of urban attractions, due to data deficiencies, it is difficult to state categorically that this has consistently been the case. In fact, at certain times, it is possible to demonstrate that the Bangladesh experience is at odds with the growing body of theoretical literature on Third World migration[2].

Our primary interest here, however, is not to isolate those factors that currently result in total migration from rural to urban areas in Bangladesh, but to deal with those which led to the sudden influx of migrants roughly between Bangladesh Independence in 1971 and the Government decision to remove the squatters from the urban areas at the beginning of 1975. Because of data deficiency problems, the primary time period for this analysis must necessarily span an even longer period: from 1961 to 1974. Certainly, as we will see, not all migrants during this period became squat-

Table 1. Population of the Largest Cities in Bangladesh.

City	1961 Population and Rank		1974 Population and Rank		1981 Population and Rank	
Dhaka[1]	521,034	(1)	2,003,729	(1)	2,365,695	(1)
Chittagong	364,205	(2)	1,061,484	(2)	1,391,877	(2)
Khulna	127,970	(4)	521,704	(3)	646,359	(3)
Narayanganj	162,054	(3)	322,921	(4)	405,562	(4)
Rajshahi	56,885	(7)	132,909	(6)	253,740	(5)
Mymensingh[2]	53,256	(9)	182,153	(5)	190,911	(6)
Comilla[2]	54,504	(8)	84,446	(9)	184,132	(7)
Barisal[2]	69,936	(5)	98,127	(7)	172,905	(8)
Sylhet[2]	37,740	(12)	59,546	(12)	168,371	(9)
Rangpur[2]	40,634	(10)	72,829	(11)	153,174	(10)
Jessore	39,304	(11)	76,168	(10)	148,927	(11)
Saidpur	60,628	(6)	90,132	(8)	126,608	(12)

Sources: Bangladesh Census Commission, 1975 and
         Bangladesh Bureau of Statistics, 1985

[1]The 1981 population of Dhaka Standard Metropolitan Area,
which includes Dhaka Municipality as given, and surround-
ing municipalities such as Mirpur, Gulshan, Narayanganj
and Tongi was 3,430,312.
[2]In the cases of Mymensingh, Comilla, Barisal, Sylhet and
Rangspur, at least some of the increase between 1974 and
1981 was due to urban boundary changes.

ters. In fact, the proportion of squatters to total migrants
appears to have been surprisingly low.

    Three sets of "push" forces can be identified that have
been largely instrumental in the decision to leave the rural
areas by large numbers of the formerly agricultural population. These are the existence of high population densities
in the rural area and the subsequent problems involved with
providing subsistence standard of living for the inhabitants, the effect of natural disasters, such as floods,
cyclones and tidal bores, and finally the disruptive and
destabilizing effect of the Bangladesh War of Liberation in
1971.

    The extent of high population densities in the rural
areas of Bangladesh are reflected in Figure 1, which shows

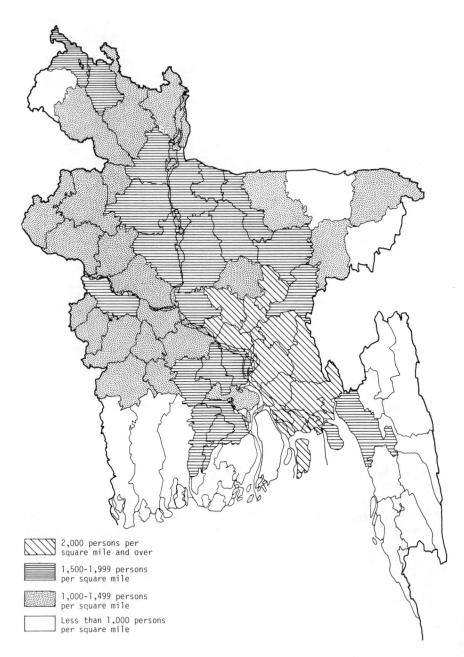

Fig. 1.   Population density per square mile (1974).

the 1974 population densities by subdivision[3]. The map graphically illustrates that in the center of the country, densities exceed 2,000 persons per square mile. Yet this center covers a relatively large area, extending from Munshiganj and Dhaka subdivisions on the west to Nardingdi on the north-east and then southward through Comilla and Chandpur to a southern limit of Lakshmipur, Noakhali and Feni.

Relative lower densities (1,500 to 1,999 persons per square mile), but still very high by international standards, extended roughly along a north-south axis, following the river systems defined by the Jamuna and Brahmapatra Rivers, but also by the Padma. The next band of densities (1,000 to 1,499 persons per square mile) were found primarily along a parallel north-south axis running down the western side of the country. These range from Dinajpur, Rangpur and Kurigram on the north, southward to Jessore and Narail. The areas of lowest densities (under 1,000 persons per square mile) were primarily found in the south among the numerous river outlets into the Bay of Bengal, in the south-east in the Chittagong Hill Tracts where densities were as low as 100 persons per square mile, and in the north-east and north-west corners of the nation.

In total, then, one can describe the density pattern of 1974 as one which peaks in the central area of the country and then generally declines as it moves out from this point. Granted, this generalization over-simplifies the actual circumstances that exist but is adequate for most purposes.

Unfortunately, in one very important sense this information is deficient. In such a country as Bangladesh the primary constraint on population growth is the available food to insure survival. This is a particularly relevant point in the rural areas where subsistence farming is the sole means of livelihood. Agricultural production in turn is dependent upon a number of factors, one of which is the availability of land which can be used for production of the primary food staple: rice. It is in terms of usefulness that the 55,000 square mile land area of Bangladesh beings to shrink.

Whereas the total amount of land in Bangladesh amounts to about 35.3 million acres, 15% is under forest and 19% is not available for cultivation. A further 8% was either culturable waste or under fallow and the balance of about

58%, or 20.4 million acres, is cultivated (Bangladesh Bureau of Statistics, 1979, p. 160). Expansion of food supplies by opening up new areas to cultivation is not one of the options open to the country as almost all of the land which can potentially be used for agricultural production is already put to that use.

At the beginning of this century, the population to land ratio was 1.3 persons per acre of cultivated land. By 1975 there were four persons per acre and it is estimated that by the end of this century, there will be eight persons per acre (Faaland and Parkinson, 1976, pp. 124-125). Yet there are wide variations within the global figure.

If one computes the population density per square mile of land actually devoted to the production of the primary staple, rice, by subdivision, some idea of the effective population density with respect to food supplies can be obtained[4]. Again as in previous calculations, the highest densities are found in the central areas. Comilla North and South subdivision, to the east of the capital Dhaka, for example, had densities of 3,116 and 3,247 persons per square mile of cultivated rice land. Narsingdi, also to the east of Dhaka, had a density of 3,284. Even rural areas well away from the major centers of population had similarly high levels of population pressure with respect to food production area. Noakhali subdivision on the Bay of Bengal had a density of 2,165 persons per square mile of rice production land, while in Khulna subdivision, the figure was 2,634.

Even in the relatively lower density areas, the area of "North Bengal" in the northwestern area of the nation, these densities were still extremely high. Although the figure of Dinajpur subdivision was only 1,543, in Bogra there were 2,119 persons per square mile of rice land, while in Rajshahi there were 1,933 and in Kushtia 1,973.

Coupled with these high population densities is a second problem and that is the yield from this available acreage of rice production land. Although yields per acre have increased in recent years, these increases have been, even with the introduction of high yielding varieties, at a very modest level - an aggregate increase of less than 15% between the average production levels in the pre-War of Liberation period, 1965-1970, and the date closest to 1975 for which data are available, 1977-1978 (Ministry of Agriculture and Forests, 1979, p. 165). As a result, rice yields per acre in Bangladesh are only one-third Japanese levels and about half the level of those in China (Alim, 1974, p. 208). Certainly rice production has increased at a lower rate than the increase in population, which has been estimated at 2.5% per annum by the World Bank (1983, p. 12).

The gravity of this situation can be seen from a somewhat different set of calculations on the acreage required to provide the average Bangladesh family with a minimum food requirement. Calculations based on the 1974 Census reveal that the typical household contained 5.6 members. Although rural households tend to be larger than urban households, assume for the moment that they are the same, an assumption that reduces to some degree the true extent of the rural food situation in Bangladesh. In order to meet minimum food intake standards it is assumed that each household member consumed 15 ounces of rice per day, suggesting that the individual rice consumption per year per family was 1,930 pounds[5]. At the time, Bangladesh rice yields were 1,154 pounds per acre (Bangladesh Bureau of Statistics, 1979, p. 165). Thus, to meet daily requirements for a very monotonous diet, this typical household was required to devote 1.67 acres to rice production. Not only do these calculations ignore the land requirements of a farmstead but also exclude the possibility of any other kind of agricultural activity. How does this minimum requirement compare with existing farm sizes in Bangladesh?

In 1977, 75% of the total rural households in Bangladesh had farms of less than two acres in size. Nearly 84% of the rural population operated farms of less than three acres (Bangladesh Bureau of Statistics, 1979, p. 144). Many of these were, of course, the rural landless. Over 11% of rural households owned no land at all while 48% owned less than half an acre. At the other extreme, 3% of households owned more than 25% of all the land (World Bank, 1979, p. 37).

From this statistical overview, it is apparent that rural Bangladesh is supersaturated with population and that although agricultural productivity has increased, and can be increased further, this sector of the economy has been a major factor over recent years in leading to rising levels of rural-to-urban migration. Even with improved technology such as that promised by the "green revolution", it is not

necessarily the rural poor with minute land holdings who
have benefited. As Stepanek (1979, pp. 80-81) demonstrates
using 1976 data, as harvests have increased as a result of
high yielding varieties, the share of income going to labour
increased by no more than 19 to 31%. Being capital- and
land-intensive, the owners of land and credit are the
greatest beneficiaries.

    Yet in addition to the economic forces which have
resulted in a transfer of the poorer rural residents to the
cities of Bangladesh over this period, a string of man-made
and natural disasters have had a similar effect. On 25
March 1971, Bangladesh declared its independence from
Pakistan and during the conflict between one and three
million people were killed. Ten million refugees fled to
India, only to return at the end of the hostilities. Industrial and agricultural production dropped to minimal levels
and the modest transport infrastructure that existed within
the nation was almost totally destroyed.

    Although the War itself came to a formal close in
December 1971, the disruption that it caused continued.
The supply of armaments that flooded the country in 1971
continued to circulate after the Pakistanis had departed.
Lawlessness, largely as a result of poverty, continued to
plague the rural areas into 1973 (Jahan, 1974) and was a
stimulant for migration from the rural to the urban areas.

    Bangladesh is also subject to natural disasters, par-
ticularly cyclones, tidal bores, flooding and droughts.
Cyclones, with winds exceeding 100 miles per hour, periodically strike the Bay of Bengal coast causing severe damage
to agricultural activity as well as the housing stock which,
for the most part, consists of a timber framework covered
with bamboo matting. The winds in turn create storm
surges on the Bay of Bengal and these, particularly when
coupled with the tide, rush across the low-lying coastal
areas potentially destroying everything in their path
(Johnson, 1975, pp. 23-25).

    On 12 November 1970, a cyclone with winds of 150 mph
devastated large portions of the belt between Khulna and
Chittagong and the offshore islands. Much of the area was
flooded with 8 to 20 feet of water with waves up to 30 feet,
and at least 225,000 people perished (Sommer and Mosley,
1973, pp. 122-123).

Although storms can destroy complete communities, cyclones are not generally thought to be large contributors to the permanent migration process, although as a short-term factor as a creator of refugees, they can play a significant role. Most population in affected areas tend to return there as soon as possible and attempt to re-establish their traditional agriculturally-oriented economic activity. Nevertheless, as can be seen in Table 2 covering cyclone losses during the 1960s, the damage can be very significant.

Far more potentially disruptive is the problem of flooding. Nearly the entire country of Bangladesh is a delta and without it Bangladesh could not exist. The river systems which lace the country provide not only the nation's transport and communication systems but also provide the area of richest agricultural land. In fact, four times as much water flows through the country as falls on it because of the size of the drainage basin of the Bangladesh rivers (Johnson, 1975, p. 26). At the same time, however, as shown in Table 3, the rains can cause widespread destruction.

The rainfall itself is concentrated in the monsoon period from May to October. During these months, the rainfall is daily and although it varies from one part of the country to another, it may be no more than one-half inch daily. The result of this rainfall, however, is to flood somewhat over one-half the total land area of the country.

The Bangladesh agricultural system is geared to the monsoon period. The aman rice crop is transplanted to the paddy fields just before the monsoon begins and then races the rising flood waters to its maturity. Once the waters recede, the harvest takes place. This particular rice crop is highly dependent then upon the timing and the quantity of the seasonal rainfall. If the monsoon comes late or if it provides too much or too little rainfall, the yield can be significantly reduced. Given the razor-edge type of existence of the majority of Bangladesh farmers, any reduction of yields can accelerate the chain of rural-to-urban migration, as emergency food relief in time of need has traditionally been most available in the urban areas.

A classic example is the flooding that occurred in the summer of 1974 which swelled not only the ranks of the urban migrants but that of the urban squatter population as well, only six months before the resettlement programs of

CHAPTER TWO

Table 2. Effect of Cyclones in East Pakistan, 1960-1970.

Year	Area Affected (square miles)	Population Affected (millions)	Loss of Human Lives	Estimated Property Loss (millions of Taka)
1960	4,160	4.40	8,150	168.9
1961	9,000	5.30	11,468	300.0
1962	...	...	...	...
1963	6,100	4.50	11,500	245.0
1964	50	0.02	196	4.0
1965	18,142	10.30	20,152	559.4
1966	4,227	3.50	850	121.0
1967	...	...	...	...
1968	...	...	...	...
1969	1,465	0.42	966	18.2
1970	3,897	3.30	265,794	887.2

Source: Government of The People's Republic of Bangladesh (1975), p. 10.

1975 began. In that year the monsoons arrived at their normal time and although the flooding seemed to be only slightly more excessive than usual in early August, by the middle of the month it was realized that as much as 90% of the monsoon rice crop might be destroyed (The Guardian, 1974). The shift from a normal monsoon to excessive flooding was so subtle that aid agencies were caught unprepared. The combination of heavy rainfalls and rapid melting of a heavier than usual snowcover in the Himalayas submerged 80% of the entire country, causing the worst flooding in 150 years.

Unable to feed themselves in the rural areas and with their houses and farmsteads destroyed, nearly 100,000 refugees flocked to 138 special relief camps established around Dhaka. Even after the flood levels receded, for many there was little incentive to return. With little or no land, coupled with the uncertainty of food supplied in the rural areas, many refugees opted to remain in Dhaka supporting themselves in any way that they could.

Table 3. Effect of Floods in East Pakistan and Bangladesh, 1960-1974.

Year	Area Affected (square miles)	Population Affected (millions)	Loss of Human Lives	Estimated Property Loss (millions of Taka)
1960	...	...	...	...
1961	...	...	...	...
1962	13,800	13.1	177	553.6
1963	14,400	6.6	10	183.5
1964	...	...	...	...
1965	...	...	...	...
1966	11,650	9.5	39	577.1
1967	...	...	...	...
1968	15,000	12.5	221	1,163.7
1969	3,000	2.2	77	82.2
1970	14,632	14.0	87	1,560.4
1971	...	...	...	...
1972	...	...	...	...
1973	...	...	...	...
1974	22,000	22.0	1,978	...

Source: Government of The People's Republic of Bangladesh (1975), p. 11.

It can be seen then that a number of factors existed during the period 1961 to 1974 which tended to push the rural Bangladeshi from the countryside and into the city. Both the landless and those who had too little land to provide a livelihood for the household and no accumulated savings to cushion the series of disasters from war or from nature, were those most likely to make the move. It appears, in fact, that it was only because the cities were not much more attractive to rural residents than the countryside that past levels of urbanization have been so low.

THE LURE OF THE URBAN AREAS

Despite the strength of the rural "push" factors that nudged the poor toward a decision to migrate to urban areas

during this period of Bangladesh history, there were, undoubtedly, strong urban "pull" factors at work as well.
Largely, these appear to have been economic. Although
their absolute strength seems to have been rather weak,
taken in comparison with similar factors in rural areas, they
take on added significance.

Although income data for this crucial period between
1965 and 1975 is exceedingly sketchy for Bangladesh, certain
wage rate series do exist which tend to confirm the general
observation that wages tended to be higher in urban than in
rural areas. Whereas unskilled agricultural workers, a category that necessarily would include the bulk of the rural
landless, earned an average wage of Tk. 5.41 per day in
1973-1974 (the exchange rate at the time was US $1.00 = Tk.
7.97), unskilled construction labour in Dhaka, such as
helpers (jogali), earned an average of Tk. 7.08. Skilled
categories in the building industry earned even more, a
mason working on one of the four "divisional" towns (Dhaka,
Chittagong, Khulna or Rajshahi) earned Tk. 13.28 while
carpenters earned Tk. 12.05[6].

During this particular period, even unskilled workers in
manufacturing received higher wages than they might have
expected with similar skill levels in agriculture[7]. Unskilled labour in the match manufacturing industry received
an average daily wage of Tk. 7.69 in Dhaka, while unskilled
cotton textile workers received Tk. 6.29 and in jute textiles
the equivalent wage was Tk. 6.30. The wages for skilled
workers were on average about 25% higher than for the
unskilled (Bangladesh Bureau of Statistics, 1976).

At the same time, however, one has to be very careful
about over-generalizing these conclusions. The newly
arrived rural migrant in an urban area was likely to
encounter difficulty in obtaining jobs, even unskilled jobs,
such as these. His entry into the urban labour market was
more likely to have been into the informal rather than the
formal employment sector. Although there was the possibility of entry into unskilled construction labour, it was far
more likely that he would end up with employment in even
less glamorous pursuits. The residual labour sector in
Dhaka during this period, and even today, seems to be that
of the bicycle rickshaw puller, where wages were lower than
would have been obtained in agriculture. As we will see, a
high proportion of squatters in Dhaka during this period

were indeed employed in this low-paid segment of the trans-portation sector.

The net result of this was that although urban incomes might have been somewhat higher than those in rural areas, the net differential was probably fairly insignificant as a causal variable in the migration decision. Nevertheless, when income differentials are combined with cost-of-living differentials, a relative advantage ironically does seem to have accrued to the urban areas. Surprisingly, it was the price of food which made life in the urban areas most appealing.

In 1943, as many as three million people died in the Bengal Famine (Chen and Rohde, 1973, p. 190). As a result of this disaster, the British introduced a food rationing system that was designed to guarantee food supplies to the poorer members of Bengali society. Over the years this social welfare measure has been expanded to include increas-ingly larger numbers of people. As a result, all residents of Dhaka, Narayanganj, Chittagong, Khulna, Rajshahi and Rangamati are entitled to a ration card which permits them to purchase certain quantities of food at subsidized prices. The amount of this subsidy can at times result in a signifi-cant boost in urban real incomes. For example, as Stepanek notes (1979, p. 71), in late 1974 the international prices of wheat and rice were US $300 and US $600 per ton respect-ively. Domestic prices in Bangladesh were even higher. Yet at the same time, the recipients of the rationing system were paying the taka equivalent of no more than US $169 per ton for wheat and US $203 per ton for rice.

The net result of this price disparity is not only to upset the cost-of-living balance between the rural and urban areas of Bangladesh but also to act as an urban pull factor, enticing further destitute rural migrants to the major cities of the nation.

PUSH AND PULL FACTORS COMBINED

Regardless of what weighting one assigns to the relative importance of the two, the net result of the rural push and urban pull factors was to drive up the urban population of the major Bangladesh cities during this period at an unpre-cedented rate. This has already been clearly seen from growth rates of the nation's largest cities between 1961, 1974 and 1981, which were given in Table 1. Over this period each of these cities grew significantly in size. This seems to indicate that in all of the cities, the change was due at least in part, and in several cases a very significant part, to in-migration from other areas. Although over this period boundary changes as well as change in the Census definition of urban areas have contributed to this gain in some cases, the effect of migration upon population levels is clear to see.

At this stage, it may be of value to examine the limited information that exists with respect to the number of migrants that moved to Dhaka during the period between the Censuses of 1961 and 1974 as this at least partially provides some explanation of the events of 1975. Although it is generally thought that the volume was greater after Independence than before it, no hard data exist to substantiate this supposition. Similarly, no fertility data exist for the residents of Dhaka prior to the 1961 Census. Although one might guess that, like in other Third World countries, urban birth rates are generally lower than rural birth rates and that long-term residents have lower reproduction rates than those recently arrived from rural areas, virtually no data are available to substantiate this. In fact, the only information available questions this "traditional knowledge". Muhammad (1974) has suggested that there was no difference between rural and urban growth rates.

Nevertheless, proceeding on the basis of the very limited amount of data that does exist, one can make a very rough estimate of the proportion of migrants to longer-term residents of Dhaka. Despite theoretical reservations, if one assumes that the long-term residents of Dhaka, crudely defined as those present in the city at the time of the 1961 Census, experienced a net rate of population increase that equalled that of the nation over the 1961 to 1974 period, as suggested by Muhammad, i.e., 2.7% per annum, then over the 13 year period one would expect the 1961 population of 521,034 to have increased to 736,685 by 1974. Then the 1974 population of 2,003,729, minus the "net natural growth population" of long-term residents 736,685, suggests that there were 1,267,044 new residents in the city in 1974 who would not have been present except for migration. This amounts to 63% of the 1974 Dhaka population.

This figure must, however, be interpreted with extreme caution. Obviously no account is taken of the natural increase of the migrant population. Certainly a large proportion of this migrant resident population in Dhaka as of 1974 were born there. Hence, the migrant population must be defined as consisting of actual migrants plus resulting families that were born of migrant parents after their move. In fact, in Bangladesh, the 13 year period between the two census enumerations comes very close to representing sufficient time to make up a new generation.

The really relevant question, and one which we will be exploring in even greater depth at a later stage, is how Dhaka coped with providing housing for this influx of new population which averaged, in gross terms, close to 100,000 per year. Here we shall only highlight certain constraints upon the housing market that affected these migrants. These include the provision of public housing for the poor in the Bangladesh context, the cost of moving into the existing housing market, the problems of building a new house and the resulting necessity of finding an unconventional solution to the housing supply problem by the migrants.

COPING WITH THE NEW RESIDENTS

Public housing, that is, housing for the general population that has been financed by public funds and may possibly be let to tenants at a subsidized rent, is virtually unknown in the Bangladesh context. Rather, the term is normally used to refer to housing provided by government and public corporations for its own employees. Even within this sphere, a relatively insignificant number of government servants, just over 3%, actually live in such public housing (Planning Commission, 1980, pp. XIX-4). Obviously if this is a government priority area where demand can be met only to such a minor degree, it is hardly surprising that beyond this group very little housing is provided. Although some minor schemes have been prepared for refugees and certain categories of the destitute, for the most part, the provision of housing stock is not considered a government responsibility primarily because the government simply cannot afford it.

As a result, given the high levels of rural-to-urban migration that occurred during this period 1961 to 1974, the options open to these newcomers were few. One option was to take over possession of existing houses or to build new ones as owner-occupiers. A second option was to move into existing housing stock which was owned by friends and relatives, sharing with them. The third option was to take unauthorized possession of someone else's land or housing and become a squatter.

The first option is one that was not really available to the newcomers. It has been estimated that in 1974 there was a housing backlog in Dhaka of 47,195 units (Chaudhury, Ahmed and Huda, 1976, p. 92). Given the relatively poor economic bargaining position of those pushed out of the rural areas, the possibilities of obtaining a unit of existing housing stock was remote.

Obtaining rental housing was an equally bleak prospect except where doubling-up could take place in the slum areas of the city. A generalized map of the monthly house rental rate for Dhaka is presented in Figure 2[8]. Although only very limited information on urban wage rates have been introduced to this stage, it is apparent that an unskilled worker earning Tk. 5 to Tk. 7 per day would be hard pressed to pay more than Tk. 40 as a rent. Consequently a rent at this level would get him little more than a shack and even this would be located on the periphery of the Dhaka metropolitan area, far from employment opportunity, and probably on land that would be subject to flooding in the monsoon season as well.

The problems involved with building new houses presents complications as well. The first of these is that of finding adequate land upon which to build. A major constraint upon the development of Dhaka is the supply of land which is above monsoon flood level. In fact this factor is one of the major determinants of land prices within the Dhaka area (Khan, 1975/1976, p. 15). Whereas low land is relatively cheap to purchase, it is obviously unsuitable for residential use.

The values of land in Dhaka are presented in Figure 3. If the newcomer wished to be near the employment opportunities available in the center of the city, areas adjacent to and to the north of the Burhiganga River, it would have been very difficult to find land at less than Tk. 5 per square foot, and more likely in the range of Tk. 20 per square foot. Thus a plot of no more than 100 square feet could have cost, in 1970 prices, Tk. 500 to Tk. 2,000. If this comprises one-third or even one-fourth of the actual housing costs, which would have provided a fairly basic one room bamboo structure, total costs could have ranged from Tk. 1,500 to Tk. 8,000 (approximately US $205 to US $1,095). Modest as these amounts are by international standards, they are expensive solutions to the housing problem in Bangladesh.

The second option open to the newcomer was to double up with someone already in the urban area. It appears that this was the most popular solution to the Dhaka housing problem. According to 1961 Census of Housing figures, there were in Dhaka on average 5.5 persons per room. The 1974 Census of Housing reveals that this figure had increased over the intervening period to 7.65 persons per room (Planning Commission, 1980, pp. XIX-10). As rooms were unlikely to be much over 50 square feet, the levels of overcrowding that were likely can easily be seen. One by-product of this doubling up was ever increasing density levels reaching in excess of 2,000 people per acre[9].

But what happens if the newcomer could not afford either to buy an existing house or to build a new one? And what if he either had no relatives in Dhaka or if they had already filled their own housing to capacity? This seems to leave little other than the third option: squatting.

At the beginning of January 1975, the Bangladesh Ministry of Public Works (1975) reported that they had removed 172,589 squatters from Dhaka. Of the total migrant population, the squatters probably made up somewhat less than 14%. Based on international comparisons with nations with far higher incomes, this figure is surprisingly low. Despite the traditions of rural poverty, the natural disasters and the effects of the War of Liberation, a very high proportion of the migrant population found living accommodation within the more formalized parts of the housing market that existed in Dhaka. Even if one reasonably assumes that in the post-Independence period between 1972 and 1974 that the proportion of squatters to migrants increased[10], one can see that they were far less numerous than in many other cities throughout the Third World. In fact, one cannot help but wonder if it was because the number of squatters was so

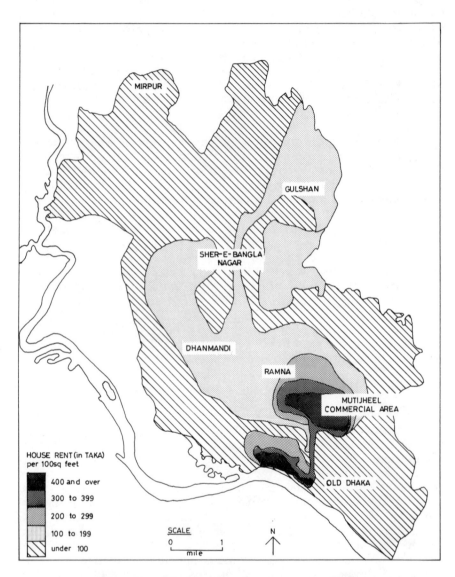

Fig. 2.   Dhaka city house rent, 1974
Source: Adapted from Centre for Urban Studies (1976,
p. 35).

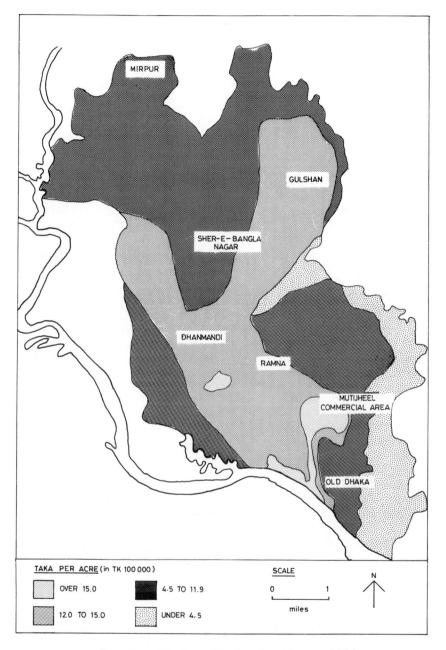

Fig. 3. Dhaka city land values, 1974.
Source: Adapted from Centre for Urban Studies (1976, p.34).

low that in the end the Government felt it was feasible to
take action against them.

CHARACTERISTICS OF BANGLADESH SQUATTERS

As noted, by 1974 about 10% of Dhaka's population were
squatters. Although the proportions were somewhat smaller
in the other leading Bangladesh cities of Khulna and
Chittagong, there was a tendency for this figure to creep
upwards, indicating a number of problems that were inherent
within the fabric of Bangladesh society at the time. In the
following chapter, we shall examine the various steps taken
by the Central Government and urban authorities to improve
the lives of these squatters. Yet to fully appreciate the
problems faced by these policy-makers, one must know
something about the circumstances of these urban poor.
Where did they come from and why did they come? How did
they live? How did they make a living?

A relatively large amount of information was collected
about the circumstances of the squatters over the three year
period from 1972 to 1974. At least three of the studies
which were undertaken can be used to provide us with the
necessary understanding for an evaluation of the policies
that were eventually proposed. The earliest of these,
published in November 1973, was a fairly small survey
carried out by the Urban Development Directorate of the
Ministry of Public Works and Urban Development (Khan and
Alam, 1973). The second, and largest of the three surveys
considered here was carried out by the University of
Dhaka's Center for Urban Studies (1976) under the sponsorship of the Government's Urban Development Directorate.
This study examined the social and economic characteristics
of squatters in the nation's three largest urban areas. The
third study referred to here was sponsored by the Local
Government Institute (Qadir, 1975) and it provides an
additional basis for comparison with the others.

One objective of the 1973 Urban Development Directorate
survey was to obtain summary information upon the major
squatter areas of Dhaka in order to assist subsequent
studies. Although it was unfortunate that this information
was not collected for Chittagong and Khulna, it can be used,
as it is here, to provide an overview of the problems faced
by the squatter communities in the capital city.

In 1973 squatters were scattered across Dhaka more or less ubiquitously; however, Khan and Alam, in the study for the Ministry of Public Works and Urban Development, identified 19 settlement clusters which had populations of at least 500. These mini-settlements within a settlement are listed in Table 4 and identified on Figure 4 by the code number of the cluster. They had populations which ranged up to 30,000 and covered anything from one-quarter of an acre up to 65 acres. None of the estimated net densities were low by any standard, yet the highest densities, 3,000 people per acre, were exceedingly high. The estimates of per capita incomes reveal an exceedingly poor population with the highest average per capita incomes not exceeding Tk. 300 (US $38) per month with an overall average of Tk. 230 (US $29) per month. Unfortunately, the sample used in this study was too small to allow much confidence to be placed in a generalization of the results.

The Center for Urban Studies (1976) information is based on a much larger survey. After estimating the approximate number of squatters within each settlement within the three urban areas, it was decided that 400 interviews would be carried out: 200 in Dhaka and 100 in both Khulna and Chittagong. This is still a relatively small sample, but it was thought to be adequate on the basis of a 1973 Center for Urban Studies survey which found that the squatters comprised a fairly homogeneous population.

As anticipated, it was discovered that the cluster settlements were poorly supplied with utility and social services. None of the ten locations analyzed in Dhaka were supplied with sewerage systems or electricity. One out of the six settlements studied in Chittagong and one of the five in Khulna had sewerage facilities while one area in Chittagong had electricity. Although drinking water facilities were generally present, they were in short supply. For example, 15 tubewells in six locations in Dhaka served 17,000 people, while three tubewells in three areas of Chittagong served a population of 5,000 and seven in three areas of Khulna served 17,600.

With respect to social services, none of the areas, despite their populations which were equal to those of fairly large towns in Bangladesh, had nursery schools, secondary schools or medical centers. Only two of the areas in Dhaka had primary schools, compared to three in Chittagong and

Tabke 4. Comparative Data on Squatter Clusters in Dhaka 1973.

Code No.	Name of Community	Population	Acreage	Net density per acre	Per capita* Income	Income Range
1	Mohammadpur	500	1.0	500	200	150–250
2	Lalmatia	2,500	1.5	1,600	175	150–250
3	Green Road	1,500	1.0	1,500	225	150–350
4	Babupara	30,000	15.0	2,000	250	200–300
5	Hazaribagh	1,200	1.0	1,200	175	150–250
6	Buriganga	2,000	1.5	1,300	250	150–350
7	Postagola	2,500	1.5	1,600	200	100–300
8	Nayapaltan	1,000	1.0	1,000	300	250–300
9	Bijoynagar	2,400	1.0	2,400	275	250–300
10	Rajarbagh	2,700	1.5	1,800	300	200–400
11	Shajahanpur	4,200	5.0	840	300	250–350
12	Malibagh Railway Line	500	0.25	2,000	150	100–250
13	Malibagh	1,800	5.0	360	250	150–500
14	Kamalapur	3,000	3.0	1,000	275	100–600
15	Palassey Railway Line	3,000	1.5	2,000	250	200–300
16	Kawran Bazar	10,000	5.0	2,000	150	150–300
17	Begumbari	3,000	1.5	2,000	200	150–350
18	Kataban	15,500	18.0	860	275	250–300
19	Rest of the Railway Line	30,000	65.55	457	–	–

* At the time of this survey in November 1973, the official rate of exchange was US$1.00 = Tk. 7.97.

Source: Khan and Alam (1973) p. 2.

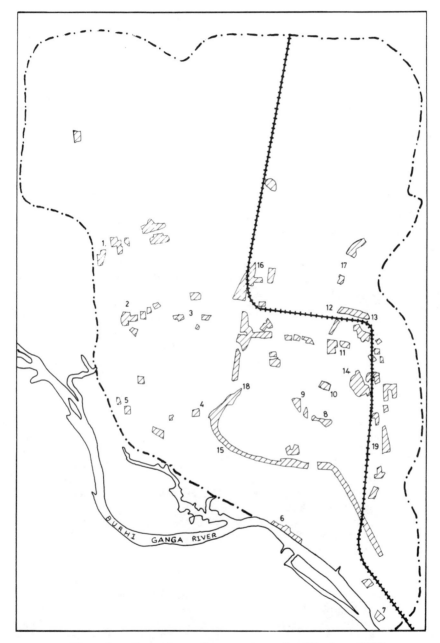

Fig. 4.   Location of squatters in Dhaka, 1974
Source: Adapted from Khan and Alam (1973).

five in Khulna. No information was collected with respect to
quality of education, whether the schools were actually in
operation or on the proportion of the children who attended
the school. At the same time, however, mosques were
present in nearly all communities.

The birthplace of the head of the family was considered
to be a valid indicator of the place of origin of the squatter
household. As Figure 5 shows, most squatters came from
areas fairly close to their squatter residences. Dhaka, with
its central location, size and employment opportunity, had
the largest catchment area of the three cities. At the same
time, however, certain origination areas provided the
majority of the squatters to each of the urban areas.
Excluding the immediate district of Dhaka, Khulna and
Chittagong, most squatters came from Comilla, Barisal and
Faridpur. As we have already seen, these areas had high
population densities. There were other common features,
however, such as communication links with the urban areas
and a location that was fairly close to the cities of desti-
nation.

For some undetermined reason, the CUS found that the
Dhaka heads of family were younger than their counterparts
in either Chittagong or Khulna. About two-thirds of the
Dhaka heads were between the ages of 25 and 44, while in
Chittagong the figure was 50% and in Khulna 52%. Whereas
21% of the Dhaka heads were over 45, in Chittagong this
proportion was 43% while in Khulna it was 39%[11].

Educationally, the heads of families were similar to the
population of Bangladesh as a whole. The majority were
illiterate although the Dhaka squatters were better educated
than in the other cities. Of the Dhaka family heads, 53%
could do no more than sign their names, compared to 77% in
Chittagong and 69% in Khulna. At the same time nearly 20%
of squatter heads of family had studied at higher than the
primary level, compared to only 7% in Chittagong and 13% in
Khulna[12].

There was remarkably little unemployment among the
heads of the squatter families. Most were employed in
informal sector occupations although there was a scattering
of workers in professional services, skilled and semi-skilled
labour and office workers. With its various administrative
functions, Dhaka claimed the highest proportion of office

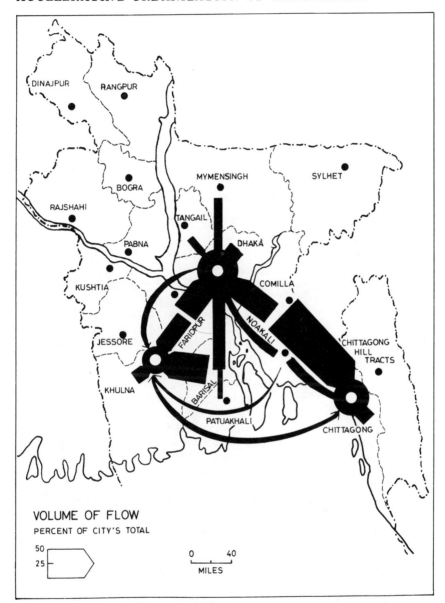

Fig. 5.   Place of origin of squatters by district, 1974
Source: Centre for Urban Studies (1976, p. 49).
The thickness of each arrow indicates the percentage of
originations of migrants to each of the three urban destinations: Dhaka, Chittagong and Khulna.

workers.   Chittagong, with its important port facilities, led
in the proportion of transport workers, while Khulna, an
industrial city, had the highest proportion of laborers.

The study sponsored by the Local Government Institute provides a more detailed breakdown of the actual jobs
performed by members of squatter families in Dhaka, including day laborers, rickshaw pullers, peddlers, maid servants,
government and private firm service workers and tech-
nicians[13].   Table 5 presents a consolidated occupational
distribution of heads of squatter families from the three
cities investigated by the Center of Urban Studies in 1974
and the Local Government Institute study of Dhaka in the
same year.

Although certain minor discrepancies can be noted
between the two surveys of Dhaka, this is probably
accounted for by the different sampling frames used by the
two studies.   The LGI study included only three of the
squatter settlements: Lalmatia, Babupara and Nayapaltan,
while the CUS survey approached a greater number[14].
The striking point, then, is not the differences between the
studies but the homogeneous nature of the settlements.

It was found that family members also contributed to
household income.   In Dhaka, for example, the CUS survey
discovered that 13% of the wives of squatter families were
employed, a third of this number holding jobs in household
and personal services.   Similarly, about 13% of Dhaka children worked, a smaller proportion than in either Chittagong
or Khulna.   Their jobs were primarily as transport workers
(presumably rickshaw pullers) and as laborers.

Information concerning income was also obtained in the
CUS study.   Although such data are probably subject to a
wide degree of error, certain points are still of interest as
this information is all that would be available to assess the
ability of squatter families to pay for housing if a more
formalized tenure arrangement were to be introduced.

Nearly all of the squatters reported that their money
incomes had increased as a result of migration to the urban
areas.   Unfortunately, given the design of the question-
naires used by the CUS, it is impossible to deflate the
money incomes to a real income basis due to the lack of data
on either the year that the move was made or the expen-

Table 5. Occupations of Head of Families of Bangladesh Squatters, 1974.

Occupations	CUS Survey Dhaka	CUS Survey Chittagong	CUS Survey Kulna	LGI Survey Dhaka
PRIMARY AND SECONDARY SECTORS				
Labourers	15.0	29.0	34.0	22.6
Day Labourers				
Skilled and Semi-skilled Workers	7.0	2.0	8.0	
Factory Workers				2.4
Masons				4.2
Technicians				4.8
Transport Workers	22.0	34.0	16.0	19.6
Rickshaw Pullers				
SERVICE SECTOR				
Hotels and Restaurants	1.0	1.0	4.0	
Household and Personal	6.0	1.0	1.0	
Maid Servants				8.3
Offices	25.0	12.0	6.0	
Services (Government & Private Firms)				4.8
Professional Services	0.5	1.0	6.0	
BUSINESS SECTOR				
Shopkeepers and Business	23.0	17.0	24.0	
Business				13.1
Shopkeepers				6.5
Peddlers				10.7
OTHER				
Beggars	0.5	3.0	1.0	3.0
TOTAL	100.0	100.0	100.0	100.0

diture pattern prior to migration. In 1974, as verification of
the earlier Ministry of Public Works study, the CUS found
that 52% of the Dhaka heads of squatter families earned less
than Tk. 300 (US $37 at exchange rates in force at the
time), compared to 33 and 35% in Chittagong and Khulna
respectively. Even when family incomes are considered, 45%
of Dhaka families still earned less than this minimal amount.

Given the low levels of income, most family earnings
were found to go on food, with about 70% of families in the
three cities reporting that they spent over three-fourths of
their total income on this item. Although most families lived
rent-free (91% in Dhaka and 74% in Khulna), 69% of the
families in Chittagong paid some rent, probably indicating at
least to some extent the existence of squatter landlords who
illegally leased out government land to the squatters.

Although in such surveys there is usually a tendency
for the respondent to understate his level of savings, it is
still significant that less than 15% of the families responded
that they had any savings at all. In fact, when asked how
they would spend an incremental income of Tk. 100, most
replied that it would be spent on food and cloth while no one
in the entire sample mentioned an increase in their contribution to savings.

The houses that the squatters lived in were constructed
of a wide array of various materials: bricks, tin, bamboo,
reeds, grass, jute stalks, wood, leaves paper, plastic and
clay. The primary ingredients of their houses varied from
city to city with the availability of low-cost building
materials. Thus, bamboo was most popular in Dhaka, grass
from the nearby hills in Chittagong and golpatta leaves from
the Sunderbans in Khulna. The floors in all three cases
were generally of earth. Whereas one room houses for the
entire family was prevalent in Dhaka and Khulna, in
Chittagong, where a stronger tradition of observing purdah
existed, two room houses were most common. On the whole,
the houses in Dhaka were small, providing no more than 250
square feet of living area, although they were marginally
larger in Khulna and Chittagong. These simple structures
were mostly constructed by family members themselves
although occasionally, hired help was employed.

The most notable characteristic of the housing was,
however, its convenience to the family's place of employment.

By combining the average travelling distance between home and work for the squatter family in all three cities, it was found that 39% of all squatters lived within one mile of their place of work while 57% lived within two miles. As a result, somewhat over 86% were able to walk to work on a daily basis, a fact which helps account for the low family expenditure on formal transport modes.

According to the squatters, their primary reason for moving to the cities was for jobs. In Dhaka, 91% of the respondents gave this reason compared to 79 and 80% in Chittagong and Khulna. Urban amenities ran a distant second in all three localities while some mention was made of education, medical care, justice and status. At the same time, there was some evidence of discontent with the decision. When asked if they would return to their villages if economic opportunity existed there, 77% of the squatters in Chittagong, 78% in Khulna and 47% in Dhaka responded that they would.

The picture that one gathers then is one that generally has emerged from numerous such studies of squatter communities in various nations. Like their counterparts elsewhere, squatters in Bangladesh cities tended to be poorly paid and lived in an environment that was lacking in most amenities. The employment that they came to the city in search of was generally in the informal sector and, if the opportunity existed, they would have willingly traded their urban life for a return to the rural areas. However, since the necessities of life took up almost all of their income and since the few who had owned land probably sold it upon moving to the city, this was not an option that was open to them. From their point-of-view, there appeared to be only one way out of this poverty trap: to minimize expenditure on housing and transport in the hope of saving enough someday to improve their living conditions.

CONCLUSION

Bangladesh, like most Third World nations, has experienced high rates of urbanization in recent years. Although the rate of rural-to-urban migration was relatively low in the 1950s and the early 1960s, in the ten year period to 1975 it accelerated significantly.

The factors which formed a foundation for this accelerating rate of urbanization in Bangladesh can be divided into the conventional dichotomy of "push" and "pull" factors. Generally, the pattern was one of movement from high density rural areas to a few, rapidly growing urban areas such as Dhaka, Chittagong and Khulna.

The strength of the push factors was greater than that of the pull factors, although the latter also played an important role. One of the most important of these push factors was the increasing man-to-land ratio throughout rural Bangladesh. As rural densities increased as a result of an ever increasing population and a limited quantity of agricultural land, the chances of making a living through subsistence agriculture decreased. One outlet from this situation was to become a landless peasant, providing labour for other producers. An alternative was migration to urban areas where, because of a lack of savings, the probability of becoming a squatter was high.

Other push factors played a role as well. The effect of the Bangladesh War of Independence was particularly disruptive. Natural disasters, particularly flooding, and to a lesser degree cyclones, also exerted a migratory force.

Although the urban pull factors were relatively weaker, the differences in wage levels in rural and urban areas lured migrants to the cities. Some evidence exists to suggest that the real cost of living may actually have been lower in urban than in rural areas, particularly for those who succeeded in living rent-free within the urban areas as squatters.

As a result of a lack of subsidized public housing, high rents and land values, combined with the low income levels of the typical migrants once they arrived in the urban areas, squatting became a fairly common way of solving housing problems in cities such as Dhaka before 1975. Although the numbers of squatters were less than might have been expected, they were still significant.

3. Government Approaches to the Bangladesh Housing Problem

Urban squatting is a symptom of a number of fundamental problems that have resulted from economic development policies in a country. Rural development programs designed to augment agricultural productivity too often have concentrated upon those who already have access to the necessary factors of production, thereby distorting rural income distributions. Income distributions skewed in favor of the rural rich as against the poor result in the concentration of land holdings among the fortunate few and lead to an exodus to the cities by the landless.

National development programs designed to give priority allocation of resources to industrialization, a traditional urban-based activity, result, if successful, in significant differences in income levels between urban and rural areas and lead to a migration of the rural poor in search of a better life. Rapid urbanization reduces the prospect of orderly urban development, with almost inevitable deficiencies in the provision of urban services, infrastructure and housing, or areas where low-cost, self-built housing can be constructed. If such industrialization development policies fail, those who have responded to the prospect of increased opportunity in the urban areas are abandoned to survive as best they can.

The existence of squatting, then, seems to be an almost inevitable accompaniment to the "development process". If development policies succeed in raising incomes, squatting is no more than a step on the way to individual fulfilment in the urbanization process. If the development process flounders, the squatter may become a fairly permanent fixture in the urban environment.

This chapter examines the development of housing policy in Bangladesh and the array of constraints upon finding a solution to the housing shortage that existed in the country. These constraints are the scope of the planning system, the perpetual shortage of finance and the attitude of decision-makers and other elements of Bangladesh society toward the housing problem.

PLANNING TO MEET HOUSING NEEDS IN PAKISTAN 1955-1970

Long before the ultimate separation of East from West Pakistan, the Pakistan Planning Commission was concerned about the housing situation in the divided state. At the same time, however, very little was actually done about it. The First Five Year Plan 1955-1960 allocated Rs. 861 million (US $181 million) for town improvement, construction of new refugee colonies, development of plots and self-help housing and for government office buildings. A few settlements for displaced persons were constructed, mostly in West Pakistan, but also near Dhaka in what was then East Pakistan. However, as the Second Five Year Plan report candidly admitted, there was a significant shortfall on all physical targets set by the First Plan except within the area of government office construction where the target was grossly exceeded. As the Second Plan report states with respect to sector performance (Pakistan Planning Commission, 1960, p. 321), "the policies proposed for the public sector were not observed, the programs were only incidentally followed and the priorities were confused because of uncoordinated implementation by the several departments concerned with the programs".

Recognizing the serious nature of the housing shortage within the country, the constraints posed by high construction costs, the rising demand resulting from rural-to-urban migration and the changing family structure, the Second Plan proposed the creation of 300,000 plots to house homeless displaced persons and others from low income groups (Pakistan Planning Commission, 1960, p. 325). It was recognized that even this magnitude of effort would not succeed in closing the gap between the supply of and demand for housing as an additional 500,000 new families were expected in the urban areas over the 1960-1965 plan period.

By the end of the Second Five Year planning period in 1965, the prophecy of failure was fulfilled since no more than 150,000 new units of housing were constructed throughout Pakistan (Pakistan Planning Commission, 1968, p. 105). Whereas the Third Plan estimated the shortage of urban dwelling units in 1960 to have been 600,000, by 1965 that deficiency was estimated to have risen to about 950,000 units. Although the Third Plan for 1965 to 1970 called for a doubling of the rate of construction of new houses, it was admitted that the backlog would almost certainly increase rather than decline over the period. The Plan proposed the construction of 292,500 new units of housing with over 70% of these expected to come from the private sector even though no more than token incentives were provided. The major incentive was a tax holiday on housing investment although this was neutralized by a low ceiling on rents. The Third Five Year Plan estimated that, based on 1965 construction costs, the resulting return on housing investment was about 5% on the investment in low income housing and 7.5% on middle income housing. Given that an estimated 72% of urban families in both wings of Pakistan were in the low income category and were considered unable to afford to own a house and that the incentives for the construction of low-income rental housing were largely lacking, it is apparent that the Third Plan's sectoral objective of giving first priority of the new housing stock to slum dwellers, lower income groups and industrial workers was only marginally realistic.

THE GROWING CRISIS IN EAST PAKISTAN

The inherent deficiencies of this national effort can be seen even more clearly if one focuses specifically upon the official steps that were taken toward alleviating the urban housing problem within the province of East Pakistan prior to Independence. As a result of World War II, the 1943 Bengal Famine and the Partition of India in 1947, a large influx of migrants and refugees arrived in the towns of East Bengal, resulting in the growth of slums and urban expansion of a totally uncontrolled and probably uncontrollable nature. In order to gain some control over this situation, urban planning legislation and urban development authorities were created throughout the 1950s. For one reason or another, these steps proved to be ineffective as a means of coming to grips with the problem.

A graphic description of the existing housing situation in Dhaka was included in the report of the Dhaka Master Plan (Minoprio, Spenceley and P. W. Macfarlane, 1959):

"Much of the residential quarter of Dacca ... comprises a congested and overcrowded mass of small, two-storey brick buildings and bustee dwellings in bad repair, approached by narrow, unpaved alley ways. Few houses have mains water; most areas are served by stand pipes at the side of the road. Drainage is primitive, and refuse is piled in heaps in the streets. Of open spaces and children's playgrounds, there are none. On the fringe areas houses are bigger; but many are now in multi-family occupation, their gardens neglected or used for bustee dwellings ..."

During the period of the Pakistan First Five Year Plan, one of the organizations established to cope with the growing housing problem was the Housing and Settlement Wing of the Communication and Buildings Department of the Provincial Government. This unit, created in 1959, was specifically charged with the task of providing ways of meeting the demand for housing by refugees and the general public. Although one can find efforts to create one-room housing for refugees in the Mohamadpur area of Dhaka as early as 1953 (Gerull, 1979, p. 17), this was the first organized effort to try to meet the growing problem throughout the province.

The net effect of Pakistan's First Five Year Plan was relatively insignificant in terms of promoting policies which would result in additions to the Eastern Province's housing stock, yet certain plans emerged for subsequent efforts. The early meetings concerned with drawing up the Pakistan Second Five Year Plan 1960-1965 resulted in the conclusion that in order to accelerate economic growth in the Province, an intensive industrialization program should be included in the Plan. It was recognized that a tripling of industrial investment would greatly accelerate the already growing rate of urbanization (Urban Development Directorate, 1968). To try to minimize the impact of his problem, the Housing and Settlement Wing initiated a program to plan and construct 17 housing estates comprised of 26,000 nucleus houses and about 10,000 building plots (Planning Commission, 1973, p. 387).

In retrospect this program, ambitious by the contemporary standards of the country, appears to have been aimed at a somewhat undefined target population. Although the initiative seems to have originated as a means of providing housing for expected industrial workers, the Housing and Settlements Wing proceeded primarily on the assumption that they were preparing housing for refugees with the allocation of certain units to local residents as a means of integrating these displaced persons into the local communities.

In any event, the period between 1960 and 1965, coinciding with the Second Five Year Plan, was a busy one at the Housing and Settlements Wing. Detailed housing layout designs were prepared for a number of areas. The most ambitious of these schemes was one planned at Mirpur, a suburban community seven miles to the north of Dhaka. As recently as 1958, this area had been primarily a forested area of low-lying land which was suitable for little other than rice cultivation. However, given the increasing pressure of urbanization on Dhaka, beginning in 1959 the Government began to acquire land in what is now Mirpur Section 12 to house refugees coming to East Pakistan from India (Sher, 1979). The Housing and Settlements Wing completed a master plan for the Mirpur area in May 1960 and then proceeded, between 1960 and 1964 to draw detailed local plans for at least some of the 16 sections of the planned community. A number of inexpensive one-room nucleus houses were constructed and allocated to refugees in 1964. At that stage, probably influenced by the emphasis on private initiatives in the forthcoming Third Five Year Plan, a further 910 acres were allocated to a private development company, Eastern Housing Limited, and an additional 600 houses were constructed for sale in 1966 and 1967.

The evidence from East Pakistan substantiates the view that the Pakistan Second Five Year Plan was indeed interpreted primarily as a housing plan. Although a newly created organization, short of staff and resources, attempting to plug the existing gap as best they could, it is also apparent that their efforts were of little more than a token nature. Assuming that the migrant population to the capital alone amounted to something in excess of 700,000, the establishment of 17 housing estates throughout the entire Province and a few additional private housing construction efforts obviously fell far short of providing adequate housing stock for this rapidly growing population.

The result of this effort during the Pakistan era has been summed up by Rahman (1970, p. 142). Noting the acute nature of the housing shortage in East Pakistan and its impact upon the recent migrants attracted into the "crazy pattern of cities", he observed that "slums are springing up all around ... Houses, challas (literally, "thatched roofs") and juggis ("walls") of bamboo, gunny bags, mud and other waste materials are coming up in large number".

THE EMERGENCE OF FAMILIAR PROBLEMS AFTER INDEPENDENCE

With Independence in 1971, the new nation of Bangladesh was at last able, after over two decades of economic domination from West Pakistan, to plan for its own future. In November 1973, the country's First Five Year Plan was published[1]. In fact, this period of time between the establishment of constitutional authority in early 1972 and the publication of the Plan in 1973 was one of feverish activity and of extremely high and idealistic hopes for the future of Bangladesh. This era of optimism extended across most economic sectors and the urban problems were not omitted.

During this early stage of Bangladesh history, however, the urban authorities, constrained by the power available to them and by lack of money, were attempting to control the growth of squatter communities by very traditional methods. Following Independence, the Khulna Development Authority cleared the city's squatters from the main highway and from along the railway line to Jessore. Due to continuing high levels of demand for accommodation relative to the supply, within one year, the dispersed squatters had returned to their original residential areas. Even though, the squatter population in Chittagong was the smallest among those of the three major cities.

Partly as a result of the War of Independence, the number of refugees and homeless people within the new nation again became acute. From 1972 to 1973, the Government constructed 27,000 housing units throughout the country. Of these 4,304 units were built in Mirpur, primarily in the form of one-room apartments in double houses (Gerull, 1979). These units were to be allocated to carefully selected squatters and then run on a co-operative basis. After about 700 units had been occupied, the entire project was invaded by new squatters and further allocation was abandoned.

Thus, despite the hopes that all past injustices could be righted and that a change of national name would transform the effectiveness of urban and housing policies, it was discovered that the problems that had faced Pakistan officials were almost identical to those that were destined to face Bangladesh officials. In fact, the new nation of Bangladesh found that efforts at urban improvement were severely constrained by three types of forces that were impossible in the short term to overcome, and have in fact remained equally troublesome to this day. The first of these constraints was the urban planning system that had been inherited with Independence, a system which might reasonably be argued to be one of the causal factors of the problem in the first place. The second constraint was the lack of necessary finance to either carry out proposals for improvement or even to operate in an efficient manner the existing urban planning system. The third of the constraints was the nature of traditional Bangladesh society, a factor which adversely affected the flexibility that was required within the decision-making process to improve the urban situation. Let us turn to these three factors before examining the impact of the First Five Year Plan on the new Bangladesh.

THE URBAN PLANNING SYSTEM

It would be unreasonable to judge any poor nation such as Bangladesh on its ability to deliver units of housing to its residents. In fact, given the wide range of economic problems facing that nation on Independence it is apparent that the actual provision of housing by the government was correctly given fairly low priority. On the other hand, given the limitations on the ability of Central Government to provide housing, it could rightly be expected that the government would operate urban development and planning

policies and institutions which would enable and even
encourage urban newcomers to provide their own housing.

The core of the urban planning system in Bangladesh
was developed in the 1950s[2]. The East Bengal Building
Construction Act of 1952 was designed to prevent the
"haphazard construction of buildings and excavation of tanks
which are likely to interfere with the planning of certain
areas in East Pakistan"[3]. Although it applied to the whole
of East Pakistan, notification by government of urban areas
to which it was applicable was required to bring it into
effect and, as a result, it was only applied to the four
divisional centers of Dhaka, Chittagong, Khulna and
Rajshahi.

The Act itself created the position of an authorized
officer, appointed by Government and responsible to it, with
the power to approve, reject or refuse any application or
plan for building construction or tank excavation in his
area. In effect, the Act represented direct Government
control over the development of the nation's urban areas, as
"building" was defined to include a "house, out-house, hut,
wall and any other structure whether of masonry, bricks,
corrugated iron sheets, metal, tiles, wood, bamboo, mud,
leaves, grass, thatch or any other material whatsoever",
while "tanks" were defined to include ditches, drains, wells
or channels.

Formal planning powers were not added to the system
until 1953 when the Town Improvement Act was passed[4].
Even then they applied only to zone plans in the provincial
capital of Dhaka since the Act created a development agency,
the Dhaka Improvement Trust (DIT) to undertake various
improvement schemes[5]. Nevertheless, the planning role
was clearly less important than the development role until
the amendments to the Act added by the Town Improvement
Ordinance of 1958. These amendments gave the DIT the
power to create a master plan for the city and brought
together the powers of planning and development control
within a single institution[6].

In effect, the 1952 Act was meant to control developments by private individuals while the 1953 legislation
provided for planned development efforts. The former
established means to control development while the latter
gave this power to the DIT.

Although the DIT was authorized by the Town Improvement Act of 1953, it was not established until 1956. Organizationally, the DIT was placed under the Ministry of Public Works. This meant that it was financially dependent upon the Central Government and in particular, especially after Independence, upon the Planning Commission, to implement its projects. For almost all of these, loans were made to DIT from the Central Government and interest was charged for the use of these monies. The DIT was prohibited from internal financing by cross-subsidization of projects, a factor which had significant influence on the organization's priorities.

Although the Town Improvement Act of 1953, with the 1958 amendments, applied only to Dhaka, with time similar development authorities were started in other areas. The Chittagong Development Authority Ordinance was passed in 1959 and the Khulna Development Authority Ordinance followed in 1961[7].

The most important urban planning agency in Bangladesh was one created not by the legislature but by government order (Government of East Pakistan, 1965), the Urban Development Directorate (UDD) of the Ministry of Public Works and Urban Development. The order establishing the UDD listed the following functions:

a)   "to advise the Government in matters of policy relating to urbanization, land use and land development;
b)   to prepare and coordinate regional plans, master plans and detailed layout and site plans of the existing as well as new urban centers;
c)   to undertake socio-economic research and collection of data for determination of the location and pattern of future urban development;
d)   to prepare programs for urban development regarding selection of sites, acquisition of land, reclamation of land;
e)   to secure approval of the preparation of plans and obtain necessary funds from the government or any other agency approved by the government;
f)   to advise the existing urban development authorities on their operations at their request".

An initial major task of the Directorate was to prepare master plans for the emerging urban areas. In this field, however, there was, and for that matter, still is, a serious problem. In the absence of legislation, none of its plans are considered to be legal documents and none of its suggestive measures are binding on anyone. It has no implementation powers itself. As a result, the plans prepared in the UDD have not been fully implemented by any authority. Further, despite the experience that the UDD had accumulated by the early 1970s, section (f) of the establishment order precluded the UDD from taking any initiative in Dhaka due to the presence of an existing urban development organization, the DIT.

In Dhaka, however, the accomplishments of the DIT at this time were less than might have been expected. A master plan for Dhaka was prepared by foreign consultants in 1958 under the sponsorship of the Improvement Trust (Minoprio, Spenceley and P. W. Macfarlane, 1959). The plan itself contained a number of rather interesting elements as it recognized that the less fortunate residents of the city were unable to afford conventional housing and proposed, what was at the time, relatively unconventional solutions. Houses built of indigenous material, such as bamboo, were inexpensive and easy to erect. The Plan report suggested (Minoprio, Spenceley and P. W. Macfarlane, 1958, p. 25) that such houses should be used on certain estates and "as an experiment, the housing authority should lay down the roads, provide the public services and construct the concrete base for the houses; after this, individual plots would be let to owners to put up their own bamboo dwellings". This proposal for a sort of early site and service scheme, like much of the Master Plan, was never implemented.

Beyond that, the achievements of the DIT include a number of road improvement schemes, some parks, the development of certain industrial estates, housing projects (usually for the more wealthy members of society) and the establishment of a number of markets throughout the Dhaka area.

As already noted, one serious constraint on the operation of the DIT was the requirement that individual projects be self-financing. As a result, the concentration of effort of the DIT was very much directed to earning as against non-earning schemes. Between 1965 and 1975, for example, the DIT spent Tk. 59.6 million on non-earning schemes such as road construction and improvements and parks but Tk.

241.4 million on earning schemes, such as industrial estates and commercial developments and the development of middle and upper income residential areas.

An example of the kinds of financial problems that arose as a result of this type of project financing is found in the development of Dhaka's Tejaon Industrial Area, which is located in the mid-eastern part of the city and is served by the Dhaka-Narayanganj Railway Line and the Dhaka-Tongi-Mymensingh Trunk Road. The industrial estate was originally proposed in 1950 by the East Bengal Communication and Building Department, which at that time was responsible for coordinating and carrying out building in the public sector. Due to severe financial constraints and lack of interest by the Central Government in Karachi, the project floundered until the establishment of DIT and the Master Plan of 1958. The Plan included the development of the industrial area on ground above flood level. A recommendation was also made for a detailed local plan to provide housing areas for industrial workers adjacent to the site. The DIT, constrained by its own financial situation, bought the residential land and sold it to developers (at cost) for the construction of upper income class housing in the Gulshan and Banani areas of Dhaka.

Two interpretations of this action can be made. One prefers to conclude that it was the financial constraints that led to this solution rather than complete disregard for the housing needs of lower income industrial workers. The effect is that aside from those workers who are willing to risk crowding into adjacent low-lying land that is subject to monsoon flooding, over half the labor force at the industrial estate must travel more than 40 minutes to reach their place of work. Such a situation results in loss of production and hence perpetuates the critical resource situation of the Bangladesh economy (Alam, 1979).

On paper, the urban planning establishment of the Bangladesh Government during the early years after Independence seems rather impressive. Institutions exist and powerful legislation is available for application. Unfortunately, the effect of the system is quite different from what one might expect. Writing about the urban planning situation in 1973, James (1973, p. 1) noted that:

"Town and country planning in Bangladesh is in its
infancy. There are no development plans for the three
major cities which can act as long-term guides for
future growth while in the rural areas there are no
plans at all and no attempt at development control.
Legal powers exist for the control of land use in
municipal areas, but they are not acted upon while the
process of compulsory acquisition of land for public
purposes or comprehensive development is slow and
painful."

Because of the complex organizational structure that
had been established by a combination of legislative and
executive orders and because the powers of the various
agencies involved were frequently shared between urban and
national bodies, until recently, few have been willing to
train for jobs in a field which existed in no more than a
marginal form in the country. As a result, in 1973, in the
two national organizations which were concerned with carrying out and evaluating physical planning, the Physical
Planning and Housing Section of the Planning Commission and
the UDD, there were only six trained planners (James,
1973). Obviously, this shortage of trained manpower was
going to have a serious affect upon proposals that would be
included in the nation's first attempt at a five year plan and
would also have the effect of forcing the government to look
abroad for technical assistance in the planning and housing
field that was to be carried out.

FINANCIAL CONSTRAINTS AND THEIR RAMIFICATIONS

If anything, the problem of finance was even more
serious as a result of a deteriorating national economic
situation immediately after Independence. At the beginning
of 1972 Bangladesh foreign exchange reserves were virtually
non-existent, placing the central bank in the unenviable
position of trying to launch a new currency with neither
reserves of foreign exchange nor of gold. Although the
reserve position improved significantly through 1972 and
1973, in 1974 the country entered a foreign exchange crisis.
Reserves fell from Tk. 2,167 million in December 1972 to Tk.
913 million in June 1974 (Bangladesh Bureau of Statistics,
1979, p. 317), reaching an equivalent level of no more than
US $40 million in September 1974. This decline in foreign

reserves was largely due to international trade conditions that were beyond the control of the Government.

As Robinson has noted (1973, p. 26), throughout the decade of the 1960s, East Pakistan became increasingly dependent, like so many developing countries, upon high levels of imports and large annual inflows of capital. At the beginning of the decade imports made up 11% of gross national product (GNP) although by 1969/1970 they had risen to 13%. Over the same period exports declined from 10.5% of GNP to 9.5%. The total result of these rather subtle shifts was relatively dramatic, as the region moved from an equilibrium in the balance of payment situation in 1959/1969 to one where there was an annual deficit of 3.5% of gross national product in 1969/1970.

Without the disruption of the War of Liberation and the loss of captive markets in West Pakistan, this situation would have been less critical. Under the circumstances it was nearly disastrous. In fiscal 1972/1973, Bangladesh's GNP was 14% below 1969/1970 levels. Within specific manufacturing industries the drop was even more significant. Although manufacturing may have contributed no more than 8% to total national production, it comprised the primary export earnings, played a leading role in import substitution and formed a vital link between the agricultural sector and the international economy. Compared to pre-War fiscal year 1969/1970, jute manufacturing output was down 30% in calendar 1972, cotton yarn production was down 48%, paper and newsprint were down 53%, cement was down 53%, fertilizer was down 15% and sugar was down 74% (Robinson, 1973, p. 13).

To compound the difficulty, the cost of Bangladesh's imports also rose significantly in the 1972 and 1973 period. The price of imported wheat, necessary because of two droughts as well as the after-effects of the War of Liberation which curtailed Bangladesh rice production in 1972/1973, rose from US $60 per ton at the end of 1972 to US $100 per ton in January 1973 to US $200 per ton by the end of 1973. Inflationary pressures came from the domestic front as by 1973 the price of rice was double its pre-War level. Most serious of all, oil price increases in December 1973 also adversely affected the Bangladesh economy and, had they not been partially offset by reductions in demand, would have cost the country $100 million annually despite its low level of energy consumption.

As a result of the reduction in export potential with the decline in manufacturing activity and the increase in import prices, the Bangladesh balance of payments deteriorated rapidly, resulting in the serious drop in international reserves.

Although declining international balances, increasing imports, erratic exports and vulnerability to the upward rise in oil prices is a situation that might very well have been expected of a poor, newly independent country in the early 1970s, some blamed the Planning Commission itself for the problems, citing as evidence unreliable forecasts and projections, and failure to secure larger amounts of foreign assistance (Islam, 1977, p. 51). Certainly there is evidence of high, yet erratic levels of foreign aid commitments throughout this period largely because donor countries were experiencing unprecedented inflationary pressures as well. Such aid went from US $756 million in 1972/1973 down to US $483 million in 1973/1974, and then up to US $1,274 million in 1974/1975 (Bangladesh Bureau of Statistics, 1979, p. 344). Whether accusations of negligence by the Planning Commission in securing funds are with or without foundation were largely irrelevant under the circumstances. Almost inevitably, based upon unfulfilled expectations if nothing else, the influence of the Planning Commission declined, with unfortunate consequences. Decisions which had previously been solely within the domain of the Planning Commission were increasingly taken beyond it. As we will see, one such vital decision concerned the fate of the squatters in the urban areas of Bangladesh, where much of the careful preparation for action that had been taken by the Planning Commission was largely disregarded at the end of 1974.

THE STRUCTURE OF BANGLADESH SOCIETY

Concurrently, there existed another fundamental problem that undoubtedly had a profound effect upon the way the decision-makers viewed not only the squatter issue but a number of other crucial economic and social issues in the new nation as well. This was the problem of class division and is basic to understanding not only the social/ decision-making structure in Bangladesh but in nearly all developing countries. Bangladesh society is comprised of a number of components. Lacking either large scale capitalist enterprises in industry or feudal or capitalist ownership in agricultural activity, the economic and political system is dominated by surplus farmers, medium and small industrialists and the mercantile classes (Islam, 1978, p. 86). The residual elements of society are the landless laborers, the small scale subsistence farmers and the industrial workers.

Even the urban middle class, composed of members of the civil service and military, academics, doctors, lawyers and other professionals, due to the agricultural tradition of the country, maintains close links with the rural areas. As a result, this part of the urban-based society, which may comprise no more than a minute percentage of the total population, maintain control over the entire system. In the urban areas, it is they who make and/or influence the decisions that affect both the national and urban economies and who own the factors of production. Their control over the rural sector is maintained through the ownership of land outside the urban areas as well as a control over necessary agricultural inputs and credit facilities.

During the early years after Independence, particularly in the period 1971 to 1975, although lip-service was paid to the concepts of social equity, progress toward it was minimal (Anisuzzaman, 1979, p. 38). There is little evidence during the period to indicate that the dominant middle classes were willing in any way to relinquish their privileged position. In fact, as Islam has noted (1978, p. 87), "the coalition of the dominant classes, urban and rural middle-classes, jealously guards its political and economic power and protects its economic privileges from inroads by the landless laborers or the mini farmers, on the one hand, and from the self-employed and the unorganized labor in the informal sector, on the other".

From the viewpoint of this particular group, the urban squatters were a nuisance and moreover posed a potential threat to the structure of the social and economic system. References to the nuisance value of the urban squatters and slum dwellers is readily found not only in newspaper accounts of the period, but also in the more serious literature on urban administration.

For example, at the conference on "Our Towns and Cities", sponsored by the National Institute of Public Administration, one speaker noted (Alam, 1970, p.89) that most houses and buildings in both the public and private sector

had an "ill kept" and "shabby" appearance. His proposed
solution was simplistic to say the least: "Laws should be
passed making it compulsory for all householders to keep
their houses and surroundings clean and tidy, whitewash or
colorwash their buildings twice a year and plant trees in
their compounds."

Although few residents of the urban areas had any kind
of toilet facilities, primarily because of the lack of drainage
and sewerage facilities, this did not prevent another speaker
(Noman, 1970, p. 195) from condemning the inevitable
alternative to the lack of such utilities: "Often it is found in
the poorer sections of the cities and the slum areas that
people, particularly children, ease themselves on the road-
side drains and lanes. This is the height of lack of civic
sense." A speaker from Khulna neatly summed up the
reasons for his antagonism toward the rural migrants (Hafiz,
1970, p. 121): "The living conditions in overcongested parts
of the Khulna town, particularly in slum areas of thatched
hutments, are almost unbearable, causing breakouts of
epidemic diseases. The present growth of Khulna is dangerous for its reputation as a clean small town."

Yet it was not only the esthetics that concerned the
observers, but also the feeling that the less fortunate urban
residents posed a moral threat to other members of society.
One participant of the conference noted (Abedin, 1970, p.
168) that "their means of livelihood in most cases are not
certainly the approved ones ... A section, particularly of
the younger elements of this floating population emerged as
desperados. Street urchins swelled the ranks of such
desperados."

In a similar vein, newspaper accounts from 1973 and
1974 provided daily descriptions to their literate and advan-
taged readers of conditions in the "city of slums". Such
reports graphically described the state of 500,000 people who
attended to the "morning call of nature in the open" (Dainik
Bangla, 1974) or the "innumerable bastee girls who were
prey to venereal disease" (Dainik Bangla, 1973).

TURNING TO OUTSIDE HELP

It was within this climate of opinion that in 1972 the
Planning Commission began its preparations for the publi-

cation of Bangladesh's First Five Year Plan. Within a certain element of the planning bureaucracy, the idealistic hope of actually solving the existing problems facing Bangladesh society were genuinely held. Yet among other elements of the establishment, any proposed change to the existing situation posed a threat to their economic and social preeminence within that society.

Reasonably enough, the primary emphasis of the first national planning exercise was to be directed toward the two primary areas of basic "nation-building" and reconstruction. The latter inevitably claimed the greatest share of the resources available because of the war damage within the transport, communication and power transmission sectors. Although the exact level of damage may never be known, the Ministry of Planning estimated (Planning Commission, 1973, pp. 284-285, 325) that 299 railway and 274 road bridges were either damaged or destroyed; and virtually the entire railway rolling stock and trucks were damaged. Electricity demand dropped from 223 MW to 30 MW largely because of the destruction of physical assets of the system.

Despite such pressing problems, however, the Planning Commission took a very wide view of the overall development needs of the country. It was realized that with the growth of squatter population within the major urban areas, particularly in the capital city of Dhaka, on any vacant land that was available, efforts to carry out effective physical planning within that city were jeopardized. Consequently, the Planning Commission directed its efforts at a number of levels simultaneously. Rural and agricultural programs were to receive attention in the nation-building exercise, but employment generation and urban issues were to receive attention as well.

With respect to one part of the urban issue, that concerned with the squatter situation: although the thoughts of Government personnel toward squatters in the Dhaka area in particular were somewhat vague at this early stage, it appears that the preferred solution included the extensive creation of "temporary settlement areas". These would have served as a first stop for the recently arrived migrants. Once an urban job was secured, the migrants would have been encouraged to move to a permanent location in the city. Government officials readily acknowledged that the necessary information required to proceed with such a project was unavailable (Zaman, 1973).

In November 1973, a three-man technical assistance mission from the United Nations Center for Housing, Building and Planning arrived in Dhaka. The mission itself was charged with analyzing the various problems of squatter settlements and slum areas within the context of the Bangladesh Five Year Plan, suggesting a planning strategy for their improvement, and identifying the activities that could be followed by Government to cope with expected future rural immigrants to the urban areas[8].

The obvious first step of the study team was to attempt to determine just how many squatters lived in the major cities of Dhaka, Chittagong and Khulna. As noted in the report, estimates of the number of squatters in Dhaka varied from 120,000 to 400,000 with a most likely figure of 200,000[9]. If there were indeed 200,000 squatters, this would comprise about 17% of the total Dhaka population, which at that time was thought to be 1.2 million. The number of squatters in Chittagong was estimated by the consultants to be 12,000 or 2% of the urban population, while in Khulna they comprised 12.5%, numbering 50,000 (United Nations, 1973, p. 6).

The Mission then directed their attention to attempting to pinpoint the causes of migration to the urban areas. These were in turn divided into two groups of factors, rural "push" and urban "pull". Included within the push factors mentioned by the United Nations personnel were population pressures within the country as a whole, the resulting decline in average landholding among the rural population, the lack of rural agricultural development programs within the nation and the recurring natural disasters that, as we have already noted, continually plague the rural areas of Bangladesh. The pull factors included the opportunities for urban employment, particularly in the service, and to a lesser extent, industrial sectors, the concentration of educational opportunity in the cities, urban amenities, particularly health care and ration cards and the sympathy of the Government toward migrants as manifested by their permissiveness in allowing the establishment of the settlements in the cities.

Among the short-term measures suggested was an in-depth survey into the physical and socio-economic conditions of each squatter community in each city. On the basis of these findings it was thought that three categories of basic solutions might emerge, associated with improvements in existing settlements, the development of site and service projects and the development of minimum shelter schemes.

Rural migrants who did find jobs were most likely to find them in the service sector, which was concentrated at the center of the urban areas. The low-cost housing they required was unavailable at these locations. Due to existing high occupancy rates, even doubling up in existing housing was impossible. As a result, the only alternative was to turn to squatting. The squatting locations were almost entirely on public land where either existing land use had outlived its original purpose, such as an abandoned railway line through Dhaka, or where master plan projects had been started but then abandoned due to lack of funds.

This complex array of factors, some of which were obviously considered at that time to be beyond the existing capability of the urban authorities, required a comprehensive Government strategy to obtain a satisfactory solution. The report of the mission divided their own recommendations into two groups: those that could be instituted in the short-term and longer-term measures.

Realizing that any type of squatter resettlement program could require several years for detailed preparation and implementation, the mission recommended that improvement in existing squatter communities be seriously considered. The object of such up-grading would be to transform them into permanent settlements. This would involve the provision of water supply, sewerage disposal, electricity, drainage, access, health facilities, schools, child care centers and an improvement in the existing housing stock. To the extent possible, these improvements should be based on self-help projects.

The heart of the short-term measures suggested was the provision of site and service schemes, serviced plots upon which the squatters would be able to construct whatever kind of house they wished. In addition to services, community facilities, such as mosques, schools, health centers, open and community space should be provided. It was suggested that the sites chosen for such projects should be compatible with the overall planned urban development and must provide employment opportunity. If the sites were far from the urban center, adequate provision of transportation was necessary.

Security of tenure was an equally important prerequisite. As the report (United Nations, 1973, p.6) emphasized, "the land should remain the property of the Government to prevent speculation and other misuse. Tenure should be granted, whether to individuals or cooperatives, on a long-term lease at a reasonable ground rent."

The recommendation of minimum shelter schemes was seen as a variation on the more traditional site and service schemes. Under minimum shelter programs, a serviced core unit, a foundation platform with roof or a one-room semi-permanent structure would be provided in addition to utility services and community facilities. This is in contrast to site and service schemes where only serviced plots are provided for participants to build their own houses.

The team recognized that adequate finance for minimum shelter projects would indeed be a serious constraint. Although much of the initial expense of such projects would have to be met by the government, the formation of cooperatives would probably be necessary as development proceeded. One suggested alternative was the creation of a community housing credit institution, an organization owned by the community to capture local savings and to serve as a channel for technical, organizational and financial resources from beyond the community. Another alternative was the creation of a government-financed "work bank" to provide tools, building materials and technical guidance to craftsmen, artisans, skilled workers and cottage industries.

In the longer-term, the report suggested a full-scale housing program for low-income groups, including squatters. The goal of the program would be the construction of a permanent housing stock sufficient to meet the needs of the urban population. At no stage did the report spell out the definitional differences between the short- and the long-term and it is doubtful, given the resources available to meet even the short-term programs if this was considered to be a serious proposal.

The recommendations of the United Nations advisory mission are important in that they drew governmental attention to the seriousness of the problem. At the same time they did little more than confirm what was already known about the difficulties involved in trying to do something constructive in such a situation. Unfortunately, the report of the mission could not be incorporated into the First Five Year Plan as the mission report appeared two months after the publication of the Plan. Still the Planning Commission was in close contact with the United Nations team during their visit to Dhaka.

Additionally, the Planning Commission itself was fully aware of the housing situation that existed, even if their fears of that situation were probably exaggerated. With respect to Dhaka, for example, the plan-makers noted (Planning Commission, 1973, p. 386) that "the current mushrooming of ... squatters in the capital city of Dacca on any available vacant land undermines any effort at rational planning of the urban community and hence poses a serious menace to urban sanitation and health. This deteriorating situation if allowed to continue unchecked will not only breed social discontent but may also threaten the stability of our urban communities."

Yet the resource situation facing the planners was extremely critical. No more than 27% of Bangladesh's urban housing could be classified as permanent or even semi-permanent. As the Plan noted that in the twelve years preceding the drawing up of that Plan, there was a need for the construction of at least 370,000 urban dwelling units and that even based on optimistic assumptions, no more than one-third of this new demand had been met, with no consideration at all for whatever backlog had existed at the beginning of the period. This suggested that the already high occupancy rate of 3.1 persons per habitable room in 1961 had further increased to 4.2, and that in low-income housing areas and in slums it was much higher (Planning Commission, 1973, p. 388). Since 85% of the total urban population could neither afford to build or to pay an economic rent for their housing, radical changes in the nation's housing policy were required.

As a means of meeting this problem, the 1973–1978 Five Year Plan proposed various housing programs for specific income groups within the urban areas. For lower-middle and middle income residents, cooperative housing schemes were proposed. For the poorer members of society, inner area low-income housing schemes were suggested, along with site and service schemes for cooperative apartments in the areas on the edges of the urban areas. The proposed site and services schemes were to include the laying of a main services network on the site, the demarcation of 80 square yard plots, the building of some "core" housing and the provision of essential community facilities, such as schools, health centers and markets.

Despite the high ideals and hopes shown by the members of the Planning Commission, the launch of the First Five Year Plan could not have been made at a worse time. Within less than a year, the Plan had run into serious implementation difficulties because of a lack of adequate finance and of trained personnel. By the end of 1973 the problems facing Bangladesh were similar to those facing most non-petroleum producing Third World nations, compounded by the lack of reserves with which to weather the international economic storm. As a result, it was development expenditure that inevitably received the cuts.

The Planning Commission discovered that when faced with higher international prices, they were caught between two very unwieldy forces. As we have already noted, foreign aid receipts in 1973-1974 were significantly below levels of 1972-1973. Export earnings could not be used to make up the gap since "in the external sector, export earnings fell short of the targets and actual volumes and spares had to be curtailed drastically to accommodate the sharp rise in prices ... The overall balance of payments came under strain, resulting in a significant drawdown of reserves and short-term foreign borrowing" (Planning Commission, 1974, p. 1).

Like most other Third World countries, and developed countries as well, the upward pressure on international prices translated itself into the domestic situation in the form of inflation. In the case of Bangladesh, in the management of public finance, revenue receipts fell short of estimates by 26% while revenue expenditure exceeded the estimates by 12%. The result was an increase in the price level of about 40% over the course of the year. If measured in terms of import prices, the inflationary pressure was even more severe, as the prices of major imports rose by an average of around 80% (Planning Commission, 1978, p. 4).

As a result of the squeeze between revenue and expenditure, development funds were largely spent on salaries of the project staff and customs and other charges for aid-financed capital goods (Planning Commission, 1974). Development expenditure in 1973-1974, measured in 1972-1973 prices, was no more than 57% of planned expenditure. Very little money was actually available for the physical planning and housing projects that had been proposed in the Plan and when coupled with the shortage in technical manpower, the result was a minimum of progress in any form in implementing the National Plan.

There is also some evidence that certain aspects of the plans may have been jeopardized by an understandable lack of patience. Plans for cooperative housing schemes were included in the National Plan. According to Islam's inside view of the Planning Commission's activities, the organization of cooperatives to build houses turned out to be a time-consuming process. As a result, the Housing Ministry, faced with strong pressures to produce houses, chose what Islam calls (Islam, 1977, p. 131) the "soft option" and decided to build them themselves. The result of this overzealous interventionism was the probable sacrifice of housing construction potential, what in the long run amounted to a missed opportunity.

As it turned out, it was not only that portion of the Plan which was directed toward housing and physical planning that ran into difficulty. By 1975 the entire national planning process in Bangladesh had come to a crashing halt. In 1974-1975, the growth rate dropped to 2% from 9.5% the previous year (which itself was still well below the target of 15%). Crops failed due to monsoon flooding and famine was not altogether avoided. The residual of the 1973 to 1978 planning period was filled up with a significantly less ambitious "hardcore plan" for 1975 to 1978. Even this level of activity proved difficult for the national planning machinery to maintain. As a result, the 1978-1980 period was filled with a stopgap two-year plan, with the five year planning cycle being initiated again for the period 1980 to 1985.

CONCLUSION

It is apparent that concern with the availability of adequate housing in East Pakistan, and since 1971, in Bangladesh, is of long standing. Although evidence exists with respect to other sectors which suggests that there was an element of discriminatory policy in West Pakistan against the East, in housing it is difficult to find any indication of this. Serious problems existed in both areas, efforts at finding solutions were frustrated. As a result we have a series of Pakistani national economic plans which, when dealing with the housing problem, were each more ambitious than the one before. At the same time, however, the critical nature of the housing situation at the beginning of each planning period became more serious with each successive plan.

Upon independence, the planning procedures in Bangladesh became increasingly sensitive to the critical shortage of urban housing and the growing inability for migrants from rural areas to make any claim whatsoever on the housing that was available. During this period, a time span which includes the studies for and writing of the First Five Year Plan and the United Nations Mission on Squatters, representing the first instance of foreign assistance to Bangladesh on the housing situation, each step appears to have been soundly prepared and deliberately carried out.

As in much of the early national planning history of Bangladesh, there was an underlying ideological fervor among many concerned with the planning process, a feeling that the new nation had an obligation to improve the living conditions of all of its citizens. Although there was an acknowledgement that resources were in short supply and that, as a result, any measures to improve the conditions of the squatters would be difficult and that real improvement might only occur over a fairly long period of time, there did exist, what was apparently, a genuine desire to make the necessary effort.

Unfortunately, the constraints which had previous restricted success in the Pakistan era, returned to plague planning efforts in Bangladesh. Both before and after Independence, the search for a solution to the housing problem was affected by a restrictive planning system which was poorly manned and meagerly financed and overseen by politicians who were overly influenced by an economically dominant minority element of the population who controlled both a disproportionately large share of resources and influence. The result then, as evidenced through what was accomplished in the national plans of either Pakistan or Bangladesh, was remarkably similar and similarly disappointing. The constraints proved stronger than the hopes of the planners.

4. The Resettlement Decision and its Aftermath

Government policies toward squatters and squatter resettlement generally reflect the political attitudes of the government and the decision-makers which comprise it. Certainly this was the case in Bangladesh. By the summer of 1974, the various political forces which were to influence squatter resettlement policy in Bangladesh were plainly apparent. On the one hand among certain intellectuals who were in a position of political power at the time, an idealistic approach was proposed in the search for some kind of a solution to the immediate problems faced by the growing number of urban squatters. This view was particularly strong in the Planning Commission, but was also expressed by certain civil servants within the Ministry of Public Works and Urban Development who were directly involved in finding solutions to the urban problems of the new nation. The position of this group had been temporarily enhanced by the report of the United Nations Mission of Urban Squatters which, while suggesting improvements that were probably beyond the technical competence and financial capability of the new Government, at least provided moral support for those who sincerely felt that a solution did exist short of wholesale use of the bulldozer.

Such feelings were not, however, held unanimously. Facing the so-called "idealists" and gaining in force as the hard problems of development in Bangladesh appeared, was another faction of the governing group where quite a different approach was suggested. Although the plight of the squatters in human terms was important, particularly to the more idealistic breed of politicians and to representatives

of various international organizations, the squatters themselves can be viewed as no more than symptomatic of the
overall political events that were taking place in the nation.
It would not be totally unfair to describe the Government's
policies toward squatters as a barometric reading of the
political, social and economic changes that were occurring in
the nation. Although a detailed analysis of the politics of
Bangladesh is beyond the scope of this study, it is essential
to have at least some awareness of this situation in order to
understand what happened to the squatters. Certainly the
political environment of Bangladesh formed an important
constraint upon the improvement of circumstances of the
squatters. Not only did it have an adverse affect upon the
implementation of the Mirpur project, but also upon other
efforts to create resettlement communities at the same time.
It is to this important area that we now direct our attention.

THE RISE AND FALL OF IDEALISM

Once the independent nation of Bangladesh was created,
due in large part to the active participation in the revolution
by the intellectual elite who in turn initially held key
positions in the Government, there was a strong desire to
right various wrongs that had been ignored in the past.
The Awami League, the political party which led East
Pakistan to independence was, in the period preceding the
War of Liberation, remarkably free of ideology. As Islam
notes (1977, p. 23), the objectives and programs of the
party were expressed in the broadest possible terms,
attempting to encompass among its members a wide spectrum
of political and economic philosophies.

In fact, the only real unifying idea within the party
was that of freedom from the political and economic domination of Pakistan. Concrete proposals for a policy that
might be pursued once the freedom from Pakistan was
achieved were minimal prior to the election campaign of 1970,
the last to be held by a united Pakistan. Although the
Awami League at that time adopted "socialism" and the
equality that it theoretically implies, as a major plank in its
political and economic philosophy, prior to that date they
had no pretension to socialism. Idealistic feelings were
expressed, ranging from calls for rural land reform to the
payment of proper wages to laborers and the introduction of
a flood control plan in East Bengal[1].

The idealist fervor of the new nation is also evident from the Government appointments that were made at the time of independence. Traditionally, the public administration of East Bengal was most frequently characterized by a single word: bureaucracy (Anisuzzaman, 1979, p. 131). Drawn largely from the upper classes of the country, the civil service of pre-independence Pakistan was composed of a small well-educated, well-paid and widely travelled group[2]. Furthermore, the civil servants were largely a power unto themselves, as they were subject to little ministerial supervision as this was perhaps the least stable level of government in Pakistan due to the frequent dismissals of cabinets and ministers that occurred during the Pakistan era.

With Independence, at least for a short time, tradition was more or less swept away. In no area of the Government service was this more apparent than in the Planning Commission. The first Planning Commission of Bangladesh was comprised not of bureaucrats at all but by four professors of economics drawn from universities[3].

This influence of outside intellectuals began to disappear as one by one the academics returned to their University posts. By the end of 1975 the Deputy Chairman and all three members were drawn again exclusively from among the more traditional bureaucrats. A number of reasons have been advanced for this return to tradition. Anisuzzaman (1979, p. 137) suggests that the combination of opposition to the theoreticians from the hard core bureaucracy, lack of support from the top political leadership and frustration with their own lack of influence over the affairs of state by the academics, were responsible for their own eclipse.

Whatever the relative weighting that one may wish to attach to the important of these various problems - the lack of internal and external resources to make fundamental changes in the nation's economy and social structure, inter-governmental problems with respect to the Planning Commission and the reascent of the professional bureaucracy - the outcome is a matter of record. Over a three year period, there was a gradual but perceptible shift in Government policy from idealism to pragmatism, from the consideration of long-run development to almost complete concern with short-run policy. Placed as they were in an almost intractable political situation, faced with economic problems of an insoluble nature, Bangladesh Prime Minister Sheikh Mujibar Rahman and his associates clearly felt themselves to be under seige.

The squatters of Dhaka, Khulna and Chittagong were merely one more manifestation of what the leadership viewed as the threat to the new nation. Subject to pressure from the upper reaches of society and the domestic press on the one hand, and the international community on the other, as manifested by the recommendations of the 1973 United Nations Mission report, Government turned to a search for a solution that would yield quick dividends in the immediate future.

In mid-December 1974, Sheikh Mujibar Rahman called a special meeting with representatives of the Ministry of PUblic Works and Urban Development where he announced that the squatters were to be removed from the urban areas. It was a decision that he had evidently reached alone and developed to the extent that, in the case of Dhaka, he was even able to suggest the specific peripheral areas to which the transfer should be made.

Various reasons have been given for the pressures that finally led to squatter removal. According to intimates of the Sheikh, the primary reason given at that meeting was that the squatters were being exploited for political purposes and that bribes were being offered to them in return for political support to the Awami League[4]. Sheikh Mujibar adamantly opposed any such possible corruption even within his own party and, overruling his political colleagues, had concluded that the removal of the squatter colonies was the solution to the problem that he favored.

A second reason given for this decision was that urban land, particularly in Dhaka and Khulna, was desperately needed for development projects and that this land was occupied by squatters. Organized propaganda against the squatters highlighted their occupation of these areas. The squatters of Chittagong had largely taken up residence on reserved areas of land that were earmarked for their use and, as a result, were exempted from the removal order.

Given the Prime Minister's decision, despite private doubts concerning the wisdom of such a policy by high-ranking officials within the Ministry of Public Works, a coordinating committee made up of concerned agencies was organized. This committee, under the chairmanship of the Permanent Secretary for Public Works and Urban Development, included members from the Urban Development Directorate and the Housing and Settlements Directorate (both part of the Ministry of Public Works and Urban Development), the Ministry of Communications, the Ministry of Power, Water Resources and Flood Control, and, on an advisory basis, a representative of the Dhaka University Department of Geography.

The coordinating committee itself had no more than started its planning deliberations for resettlement of the squatters when it was overcome by events quite unrelated to the squatters but nevertheless destined to sweep them up with its momentum. On 28th December 1974, Prime Minister Mujibar Rahman proclaimed a State of Emergency. "In view of the grave situation created by hostile elements acting in collusion with the collaborators of the Pakistan Army, extremists and enemy agents in the pay of foreign powers", as the Home Ministry spokesman put it (Manirazzaman, 1975, p. 124), all fundamental rights conferred by the constitution were suspended for an indefinite period. In the macropolitical sense, the next eleven months were to be filled with frenzied activity highlighted by the introduction of a presidential one-party system in January, a coup which resulted in the death of Sheikh Mujibar in August and a series of coups in November which eventually, under the leadership of the late Major-General Ziaur Rahman, led to a return of at least a form of stability.

Although the environment of emergency was not conducive to finding anything approaching the best solution to the squatter dilemma, the committee did the best it could under the circumstances. That "best", derived under conditions of relative secrecy, was anything but adequate.

The five sites suggested originally by the Prime Minister turned out to be an unfortunate series of choices. The alternative accommodation for the squatters was to be provided at sites located in Tongi, Demra, Mirpur, Fotulla and Jinzara. These are shown in Figure 6.

The 100 acre site in Tongi was little more than a piece of unimproved swampland that had previously been designated by the Dhaka Improvement Trust's Master Plan of

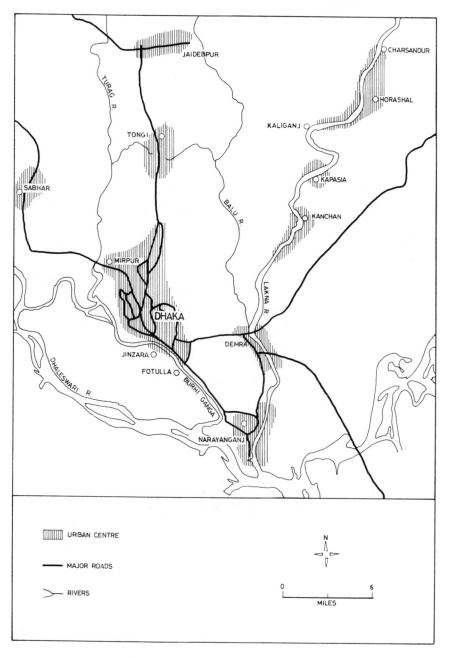

Fig. 6.   Dhaka Regional Map.

Dhaka for industrial workers' housing at the Tongi industrial estate.   Tongi itself is a thriving industrial center located about fifteen miles north of Dhaka.

The designated 103 acre site at Demra was only marginally better.   It was located near the village of Chanpara on the Lakna River about ten miles to the east of Dhaka on land that had originally been acquired by the Dhaka Water and Sewerage Authority (WASA) as a site for water treatment plant.   WASA itself had already raised most of the land on the site to above monsoon flood level.

The Mirpur site consisted of 88 acres at Bashantek, on the outskirts of Mirpur.   The land upon which the community was to be located was a part of the Dhaka Military Cantonment.   Although the straight line distance between Bashantek and downtown Dhaka is little more than five miles, due to the restricted access to the military land south of the proposed settlement, the actual travel distance to Dhaka is somewhat over ten miles.   The use of this particular land for the squatter resettlement scheme was unpopular with the military because it was from this tactical site that, in 1971, the Indian/Mukti Joddha (Freedom Fighters) artillery bombarded Dhaka and the Pakistan military strongholds to the north of the city.   There seemed to be fear that the squatters might decide to treat the military in an equally inhospitable manner.   As a result, Bashantek was considered from the beginning to be a temporary settlement site.   The permanent site was to be adjacent to Mirpur, about two miles to the east of the original location.

Another more immediate reason has also been suggested for the change in location of the Mirpur camp.   Seven months after the Bashantek area was designated as a resettlement camp it was discovered that the topological maps which were used to delineate the camp area, maps which dated back to the British colonial days, were incorrect. Areas defined by contours which should have been free from monsoon flooding were discovered to be submerged when the summer rains reached their peak.   Even by Bangladesh standards, the original Bashantek site in its original form was inadequate as a residential area.

The remaining two sites were at Fotulla and Jinzara. Fotulla is located ten miles to the south of Dhaka along the main road to the industrial center of Narayanganj.   Largely protected from flooding by dikes which comprise the Dhaka-Narayanganj-Demra flood control and irrigation project, a continuing controversy has raged since the project was completed in 1968 as to whether the area should have been preserved for agriculture or allowed to develop into an urbanized extension of Dhaka.

Jinzara is located just across the Bari Ganga River from Dhaka with access to the main market centers of Old Dhaka by boat. Given its locational and transport advantages, a number of informal manufacturing enterprises have grown up in the area. At the same time, migrants have settled in the area and the 1974 Census revealed that the density of the area was already 10,237 persons per square mile.

Although Fotulla and Jinzara were listed as among the five resettlement sites, strong opposition was expressed towards using them in the Coordination Committee meetings. The focal point of the opposition was from the Dhaka Improvement Trust who foresaw important alternative uses for both sites[5]. As a result, both locations were designated as reserve rather than primary sites for resettlement camps.

Given the nature of the sites as well as the prospect that the time for preparation was short, the Coordination Committee directed its efforts toward providing the most necessary infrastructure at each of the sites and little else. Consultants were retained to prepare layout plans giving a demarcation of individual plots, road alignments and the location of common facilities (Ministry of Public Works and Urban Development, 1975, p. 2).

As soon as rough plans were available, construction of minimum basic needs items was begun, including trench and borehole latrines, tubewells and certain necessary administrative structures, such as management sheds for registration of the squatters, a building for Red Cross activities and one for the police. Approach roads of brick pavement were also constructed to fulfil minimum requirements.

In addition to the layout plans for each camp, a rough costing was provided of the various items to be included in each. This list of costings of the preliminary "basic needs" items is shown in Table 6. The most apparent conclusion that emerges from the Table is the pronounced disparity that

existed between the planned spending on the three sites.
The Government planned to spend over three times more on
the site at Tongi than on the one at Mirpur, with Demra
receiving over twice the initial investment of Mirpur.
Assuming that the costs were to be eventually spread over
4,000 plots, the modest nature of the planned expenditure at
all sites is noticeable.

By far the largest expenditure was to be on sanitation
facilities, particularly the borehole and trench latrines.
Even here, however, far greater effort was obviously
planned at Tongi and Demra than at Mirpur. It is apparent,
and in view of later experience, ironic that the camp at
Mirpur was viewed as little more than a temporary site to be
used until a permanent location could be developed.

Over the longer term, the Coordinating Committee
expected the resettlement areas to develop into thriving
urban extensions of Dhaka, complete with community facilities, the necessary urban infrastructure and even opportunities for local employment. An outline for the long-term
plans were included in the Bangladesh National Report for
the 1976 Habitat Conference in Vancouver and is reproduced
here as Table 7. Again, note that although the facilities
which were to be constructed at the camps located at Tongi
and Demra were worked out in some detail, due to the
already apparent pressure to transfer the Bashantek camp to
another part of Mirpur, facilities for this later site were
included in no more than outline form.

The detailed expenditures for all three sites were,
however, estimated by the Coordinating Committee prior to
the transfer of the squatters, and these are presented in
consolidated form in Table 8. On the assumption of eventual
provision of 4,000 plots at each location, it becomes apparent
that the site at Mirpur has moved from being the least to the
most expensive of the three locations. This is entirely due
to the high cost of land in the Mirpur area, an area that is
far more central to Dhaka than either of the sites at Tongi
or Demra. Whereas an acre of land at the Tongi site and
Demra were each valued at Tk. 75,000 (US $9,316), land at
Mirpur was valued at Tk. 600,000 (US $74,534) per acre.
Given the requirements for 100 acres at Tongi, 75 acres at
Demra and 68 acres at Mirpur, the result was that Mirpur
became the highest cost site of the three camps. If land
cost is excluded, a perfectly justifiable exclusion since the

cost of land does not constitute an economic cost to the project, the Mirpur regains its position as the lowest cost site among the three.

The very rough nature of the cost estimates is also apparent from Table 8. The cost of the community facility buildings and the provision of the water supply were each assumed to be identical at all three sites, despite the distinct nature of their various locations. Demra, for example, is located on an island in the Lakna River. Similarly the cost of surface drainage at Demra and Tongi is assumed to be identical while drainage at Mirpur is somewhat less. Based as these estimates were on unit costs and rough measurements from the plan, it is apparent that the possibility of a wide margin of error is incorporated into these estimates. To compensate for this, the estimates include rather a large allowance for contingency costs, establishment costs and overheads. Combined, these categories amount to about 15% of the total cost of the projects.

The State of Emergency declared on 28 December 1974 was not directed at the squatters themselves, but it provided a legal instrument that could be used for their removal. Under the terms of the Emergency, the right of any person to approach any court for enforcement of fundamental rights guaranteed by the Constitution was suspended. As a result, there was little possibility of stay orders on eviction from unauthorized settlements.

On 1 January 1975, the Government announced that the squatters of Dhaka and Khulna had three days to vacate their homes. The following day, an order was issued from the Ministry of Public Works and Urban Development that[6] "all areas in the urban area unauthorizedly occupied should be cleared immediately". With the expiration of the three day deadline on 4 January, Government personnel, accompanied by police and the military went to the squatter areas and after formally requesting that they abandon the sites, began to dismantle the houses, shops and workshops (Bangladesh Times, 1975a).

At a press conference on 9 January, The Minister of Public Works and Urban Development announced that the initial phase of the squatter clearance program had been completed and that on the next day the "Clean the City Drive" would enter its second phase, that of removing the

Table 6. Cost of Emergency Provision of Infrastructural and Other Items at Squatter Resettlement Camps(1).

Category of Expenses	Tongi	Demra	Mirpur
Planning, including surveying and demarcation of facilities	Tk. 30,000 ($3,727)	Tk. 86,479 ($10,743)	Tk. 150,485 ($18,594)
Structures and construction equipment	Tk. 592,838(2) ($73,644)	Tk. 443,510(6) ($55,094)	Tk. 217,667(8) ($27,039)
Land filling	Tk. 628,229 ($78,041)	–	–
Roads	Tk. 332,686 ($41,174)	–	–
Drainage	Tk. 103,348 ($12,838)	–	–
Latrines	Tk. 1,237,033 ($153,669)	Tk. 1,096,580 ($136,221)	Tk. 336,366 ($41,785)
Water supply (tube-wells)	Tk. 428,752 ($53,261)	Tk. 448,404 ($55,702)	Tk. 319,788 ($39,725)
Miscellaneous	Tk. 72,836(3) ($9,048)	Tk. 124,801(7) ($15,503)	–
Contingency and overheads	Tk. 514,715(4) ($63,940)	Tk. 330,516(4) ($41,058)	Tk. 153,902(4) ($19,118)
Total	Tk. 3,940,437(5) ($489,495)	Tk. 2,530,290 ($314,322)	Tk. 1,178,208 ($146,361)

Cost per planned plot	Tk. 985 ($122)	Tk. 633 ($79)	Tk. 295 ($37)

NOTES:

(1) Foreign exchange equivalents based on exchange rate US $1 = Tk. 8.05.

(2) Structures included at Tongi were two administrative sheds, a Red Cross shed and one for the Save The Children Fund, a social welfare office, a police shed, a food distribution office with warehousing facilities, a milk shed, a temporary mosque and concrete platforms and covered tin shed for shops.

(3) This item included the cost of transferring certain squatters from Tongi to Mirpur, the shifting of certain huts in areas vulnerable to flooding and the cost of emergency lighting.

(4) This is the combined total of two categories of cost which were included as acknowledgement of the possible error that might have been included in the calculations. Contingency expenses were based on $7\frac{1}{2}\%$ of estimated expenses while overheads were computed on the basis of 7% of estimated expenses plus contingencies.

(5) This total is slightly at variance with the original calculations of the Ministry of Public Works and Urban Development, who estimated a cost at Tongi of Tk. 3,938,116 ($489,207). This minor discrepancy appears to be due to an adding error in the original calculations.

(6) Structures to be constructed at Demra include sheds for a health center, the Red Cross, a hospital, the police, food distribution plus warehousing facilities, a registration center, a milk feeding station and a mosque.

(7) This category includes the cost of transporting the squatters from the ferry ghat at Demra to the site of Chanpara, the expense of hiring a microphone-sound system and the transfer of Government materials from Dhaka to Demra.

(8) At Mirpur, these costs included those for a temporary administrative shed, a Red Cross shed, a temporary hospital, a food office and a temporary police station.

Table 7.   Provision of Facilities and Service Utilities for
           Rehabilitation of Squatters.

Provision of Items	No. and Location of Resettlement Projects		
	Tongi	Demra	Mirpur
1 Plots	4063	4000	4000
2 Size of individual plots	13'x25'	14'x26'	
3 Educational facilities:			
a) Primary school	5	5	Provisions likely
b) High school run on			to be similar in
2 shifts, for boys			this area as well
and girls	1	1	
c) Vocational school	1	1	

4 Health facilities:
   Maternity-cum-health
   centre
	1	1	

5 Water supply: Present no. of tubewells	80	80	
Future arrangements	Piped water from over head tanks		
6 Sanitation arrangements: Future provision	Septic tank with partial sewerage system		
7 Open space and rec- reational facilities:			
a) Central park and playground	1	1	
b) Playground with school	6	6	
c) Cinema	1	1	
d) Water front	lake	river	
e) Graveyard	1	1	
f) Religious place of worship	1 mosque	1 mosque	
8 Shopping and central commercial zone	1	1	
Corner shopping	4	4	

9 Employment opportunities:
   Small scale industrial
   plots
	137	66	

Source: Chaudhary, Ahmed and Huda (1976, p. 114).

remaining unauthorized structures and the ejection of illegal residents of houses in Mohammadpur, Mirpur and others parts of Dhaka. The Government, he pointed out, had maintained its "sympathetic" attitude towards the squatters, providing transport and assistance to move them and all of their possessions to the resettlement camps. Transportation from the camps to places of work in the city was to be provided at concessional rates to minimize the disruption they had experienced (Bangladesh Times, 1975b).

The Ministry of Public Works which was in overall charge of the clearance program kept a complete record of the operation in Dhaka which reveals (Ministry of Public Works and Urban Development, 1975, p. 1) that of the 172,589 squatters who occupied 24,757 shacks at 119 locations, only about 14,860 families were shifted to the squatter resettlement camps: 5,380 to Tongi, 5,480 to Demra and 4,000 to Mirpur. Of this number 1,381 families from Tongi and 670 from Demra were shifted to housing areas reserved for the homeless in other parts of Mirpur and something over 1,800 families left the camps for unknown destinations. Hence by the end of the operation, 4,063 families had been transferred to Tongi, 3,871 to Demra and 3,044 to Mirpur. Based upon the financial accounting of the operation, it is known that the Ministry of Public Works paid for, and presumably had the services of 3,681 trucks and 29,844 man-days of skilled and unskilled labor to carry out the transfer.

These official accounts of the squatter clearance program of January 1975 give little feeling for any human misery caused by its transfer. They do not begin to describe the passions that were aroused when members of the militia encountered armed squatters who were determined to defend their humble houses at all costs. In fact, throughout the official description of the operation, only one short statement (Ministry of Public Works and Urban Development, 1975, p. 1) begins to capture the feelings that were generated, although even then only from the viewpoint of the removers rather than of the removed: "During forceful eviction there were risks of danger and in some places unauthorized occupants obstructed with deadly weapons."

Yet in comparison with the conditions that were to be endured in the resettlement camps themselves, the removal phases of the operation appear in hindsight to be remarkably

Table 8. Planned Infrastructural and Other Expenses at Squatter Resettlement Camps, Phase II(1).

Category of Expense	Tongi	Demra	Mirpur
Community facility buildings(2)	Tk. 5,790,000 ($719,255)	Tk. 5,790,000 ($719,255)	Tk. 5,790,000 ($719,255)
Water supply	Tk. 7,314,750 ($908,665)	Tk. 7,314,750 ($908,665)	Tk. 7,314,750 ($908,665)
Sanitary arrangements	Tk. 8,300,000 ($1,031,056)	Tk. 8,020,000 ($996,273)	Tk. 5,800,000 ($720,497)
Surface drainage	Tk. 3,000,000 ($372,671)	Tk. 3,000,000 ($372,671)	Tk. 2,500,000 ($310,559)
Electricity	Tk. 2,387,000 ($396,522)	Tk. 2,170,000 ($269,565)	Tk. 1,970,000 ($244,720)
Roads and transport facilities	Tk. 11,587,500(5) ($1,439,441)	Tk. 10,662,500(6) ($1,324,534)	Tk. 7,260,000(5) ($901,863)
Site improvement	Tk. 12,523,500 ($1,555,714)	Tk. 7,514,100 ($933,429)	Tk. 10,219,176 ($1,269,463)
Miscellaneous	-	Tk. 385,100(7) ($47,839)	Tk. 200,300(7) ($24,882)
Sub-total	Tk. 50,902,750 ($6,323,323)	Tk. 44,856,450 ($5,572,230)	Tk. 41,054,226 ($5,124,786)
Contingency and overheads(3)	Tk. 7,648,139 ($950,079)	Tk. 6,739,680 ($837,227)	Tk. 6,168,397 ($766,260)

Sub-total	Tk. 58,550,889 ($7,273,402)	Tk. 51,596,130 ($6,409,457)	Tk. 47,222,623 ($5,866,164)
Land	Tk. 7,500,000 ($931,677)	Tk. 5,625,000 ($698,758)	Tk. 40,800,000 ($5,068,323)
Grand total	Tk. 66,050,889 ($8,205,079)	Tk. 57,221,130 ($7,108,215)	Tk. 88,022,623 ($10,934,487)
Cost per unit (excluding contingency, land)(4)	Tk. 12,726 ($1,581)	Tk. 11,214 ($1,393)	Tk. 10,263 ($1,275)
Cost per unit (excluding land)(4)	Tk. 14,638 ($1,818)	Tk. 12,899 ($1,602)	Tk. 11,806 ($1,467)
Total cost per unit	Tk. 16,513 ($2,051)	Tk. 14,305 ($1,777)	Tk. 22,006 ($2,734)

NOTES:
(1) Foreign exchange equivalents based on the then current rate of exchange: US $1 = Tk. 8.05.
(2) As enumerated in Table 7.
(3) As in Table 6 this category is a summation of contingency and establishment costs and overheads. It is included to compensate for possible acknowledged errors in the estimates. Contingency and establishment costs are computed on the basis of $7\frac{1}{2}$% of estimated costs while overheads are 7% of estimated plus contingency costs.
(4) These per unit costs are based on the original plans to include 4,000 household units at each of the three sites.
(5) Includes internal roads plus a bus stop facility.
(6) Includes Tk. 200,000 ($24,845) for construction of a ferry ghat.
(7) At both Demra and Mirpur, allowance is made for the shifting of squatters from one area to another.

humane. It is to these conditions that we now direct our
attention, attempting to follow through the various processes
that were followed to transform them from what were virtually unimproved swamps to habitable communities.

INITIAL CONDITIONS AT THE RESETTLEMENT CAMPS

As we have seen, the squatters were transferred to
three peripheral sites with whatever they could salvage from
their previous residences. The transfer itself took place in
the middle of the Bangladesh winter. Although this winter
is mild by most standards, for the resident population,
accustomed as they were to warmer temperatures and their
squatter shelters, the lack of protection obviously became a
threat to health and even life.

The situation at Tongi was, unfortunately, typical of
the provision of service that was provided. Water and
sanitation facilities, which were to be provided by Government, offer scope for comparing plans that had been made
against what was achieved. Obviously, the difference
between these two sets of figures reveals the critical situation in which the resident population found themselves.

By mid-January, the Government intended to provide
sixty tubewells, sixty four-unit latrines and thirty kutcha
("unpaved") or trench latrines at Tongi. The actual
accomplishments by 17 January were the sinking of twenty-
nine tubewells, the construction of twenty-one four-unit
latrines and the building of thirteen kutcha latrines
(Bangladesh Times, 1975c). With a resident population of
approximately 20,000, this amounted to, for example, one
tubewell for every 700 residents. As such tubewells can be
sunk by two or perhaps three workers within a day, it gives
some idea of the resources and effort that had been devoted
to the preparations.

Similar situations existed at other camps. In February,
a Western newspaper correspondent (The Guardian, 1975)
visited the camp at Demra and reported:

"Officials prepared for the forced migration only by
demarcating plots of land and building a few latrines
and water pumps. Now the latrines are full and no
longer usable, the camp smells of excrement. Most

water pumps do not work. Many residents have not registered and do not qualify for the food rations meted out in increasingly small amounts each day. The camp graveyard is already filled with the bodies of about 50 old people and babies who have died from disease and starvation."

The health hazard was serious throughout the early months of 1975. Coincidentally, the resettlement program was carried out during the last major smallpox epidemic in Bangladesh. Squatters who fled from Dhaka to their own villages spread the disease to at least nine other districts of the country. By mid-January, at least five residents of the Tongi settlement had died of the disease (Bangladesh Times, 1975c). That camp was also struck by an epidemic of measles which took the lives of a number of babies. As one resident recalled[7]:

"There were a lot of deaths every day. We wrapped them in newspapers and buried them together. You ask why there were so many deaths - well I will tell you why. If you are dumped in a place where you don't have means of life support: no food, no shelter and winter nights without sufficient clothes, you are destined to die."

Although efforts were made to vaccinate the residents of the camps, virtually no other medical assistance was available. At Demra it was reported (The Guardian, 1975) that the "only medicine stocked at the camp dispensary was a package of vitamin pills so spoiled they stuck firmly together, some vaccine and a few bandages".

One of the more serious disruptions that occurred as a result of the resettlement concerned the accessibility to employment. Initially, the Government committee responsible for planning the resettlement process had intended to provide subsidized bus transportation between the camps and the inner city employment opportunities in Dhaka. This was to be the responsibility of the Ministry of Communications. That Ministry was, however, reluctant to pay for it and, as a result, the bus service survived for only a few days and then totally disappeared[8].

As a result, the situation became even more critical. As we have already noted, unemployment among the squatters prior to their resettlement was relatively low. Given the opportunity to squat where they wished, there had been a natural tendency to settle near areas of employment opportunity, normally in inner city areas near jobs in the informal sector. The resettlement completely disrupted this arrangement.

The Government's planning committee had foreseen this problem and, as a result, a deliberate "decanting" policy had been followed in allocating squatters to the three camps. Squatters who had any kind of industrial experience were automatically transferred to the camps at Tongi and Demra which were within proximity to industrial jobs. Mirpur, in that case, became the residual site, a factor which might account for the lower per capita investment in the infrastructure. It might also account for some of the subsequent problems which occurred at that location and will form the basis of the case study which begins in the next chapter.

Our previous examination of the characteristics of the squatters in Dhaka in Chapter 2 revealed that very few of them had any experience at all in the formal industrial sector. The decanting policy followed by the committee was in all probability appropriate for no more than a very small minority of Dhaka's squatter population.

Once the subsidized bus service stopped running, not only was there a reduction in accessibility to job opportunities and a subsequent reduction in income, but also a reduction in the possibility of part-time employment of members of the household other than the head. Income from jobs that could be obtained in Dhaka was further eroded by the cost of commuting from the peripheral resettlement sites an the downtown areas of the city. As one resident reported (Khan, 1979, p. 37):

> "I go to Dacca to pull a rickshaw. It costs 4 taka to commute to and from Dacca. It is better I leave my family here and stay in Dacca. I sometimes visit them. I was working as a rice-seller and was doing quite well previously. There are lots of openings in Dacca. I never thought I would have to drive a rickshaw but that is what I am doing."

What we have seen then appears to have been a near complete breakdown in the governmental planning process of resettlement camps during the early months of 1975. Committees were formed, consultants were hired, quasi-plans of a rough nature were drawn, even finance was arranged, but very little implementation of these plans was actually carried out by the time of the squatters' transfer. As one newspaper observed with respect to the Demra camp (The Guardian, 1975):

"The suffering here has not been prompted by food shortage. Instead it seems the result of the absence of planning and official indifference to the fate of these people. International voluntary agencies which could be expected to help were not even informed of the camp's existence until after it was opened. No agency is as yet involved."

Fortunately, the international non-governmental agencies got involved in assisting these camps and in some cases, virtually operated them. It is to this relatively informal sector of the aid granting organizations that we now direct our attention.

THE ROLE OF NON-GOVERNMENT ORGANIZATIONS

From an early stage, the international voluntary organizations and Non-Government Organizations (NGOs) assisted the residents of the resettlement camps. Although a number of NGOs decided independently to provide whatever help they could to the resettlement camps, there was no more than informal coordination among them. As a result, there was over-concentration in some areas of need and a dearth of activity in others.

At Tongi, a choice of services was available to the residents of the camp. Terres-des-Hommes International Federation began feeding 3,000 children in early 1975. The Christian Health Services Bangladesh and the Seventh-Day Adventists also ran feeding programs to supplement the programs operated originally by the Government.

Christian Health Services Bangladesh opened a free medical clinic and a limited family planning service.

Primary schools for 1,200 children were provided through the joint efforts of the Salvation Army and Terres-

des-Hommes.   Terres-des-Hommes started vocational training
centers that were attached to the primary schools where 125
men, women and children learned tailoring, cycle repair,
jute, bamboo and cane work, carpentry and pisciculture.
Christian Health Services started vocational training in
conjunction with their health center where 50 widows could
learn cane and jute work.   In each case, modest monthly
payments were made to participants on the vocational training program.

Assistance in building houses was provided jointly by
the Salvation Army and Terres-des-Hommes.   Christian
Health Services started a housing repair program.   OXFAM
undertook the construction of public lavatories.

As the Tongi site was little more than a swamp at the
time the residents were moved into the camp, in March 1976,
the South American Baptist Mission, Terres-des-Hommes and
the Salvation Army sponsored an earth-filling program.   In
addition to improving the topography of the site, the project
provided work for 2,520 laborers, 546 of them women.

Criticism has, in the past, frequently been directed at
NGOs suggesting that they were more concerned with relief
operations of the "soup kitchen variety" than in providing
more significant and long-lasting benefits to recipients.   The
organization themselves recognize the inherent problems in
the work that they carry out.   As Campbell states (1981, p.
5), speaking of his own experience as OXFAM Field Director
in Bangladesh from 1976 to 1980, "in the light of the limited
resources available to field staff, they can face a considerable dilemma: the choice between "rescue" aid which
saves lives in the short term but may "solve" nothing, and
"development" which in some cases may fail to achieve its
objectives".

Shakur has investigated the attitudes of government
officials toward the activities of the NGOs which were
involved in assisting the resettlement camp residents.   His
analysis (1984) reveals that Government politicians, for
example, while acknowledging the generosity of personnel
from the various NGOs toward the squatters, felt that too
often they operated in complete isolation from the government.   They were critical of the efforts of the NGO
personnel to view their involvement on a longer-term basis,

suggesting that this may even be responsible for attracting further poor migrants to the city.

Despite this criticism from government officials, some of the voluntary organizations made a deliberate attempt to shift from short- to longer-term programs, taking on more comprehensive responsibilities toward the improvement of the settlement camps. Campbell suggests this is due to three reasons. First the voluntary organizations fear that recipients might come to depend too much on such programs. Second, at least in the case of OXFAM, there has been a trend toward more politically oriented field workers, leading to a greater awareness of the need to change society rather than merely adapt to it. Finally, the type of emergency that requires relief activities occurs only rarely and then does not last forever. As a result, to fully occupy its resources and personnel, NGOs necessarily find themselves involved in the longer-term investment programs.

This mix of relief and development policies on the part of the NGOs is illustrated by the case of Tongi. The residents of these camps were moved to peripheral areas but were not given agricultural land to facilitate their survival. This is hardly surprising since the people involved were city residents, and many had been such for a considerable period of time. As a result, food was one of the primary problems facing the resettled people upon their arrival at the camps.

Initially, the Government attempted to provide feeding programs but with time, a mere matter of weeks, these became increasingly inadequate. The NGOs moved in to fill the gap as we have already seen in the Tongi context. Yet their activities were not limited to those of the day-to-day subsistence type.

Once the problems of assuring survival were met, the organizations moved into children's education programs and vocational training. House building and repair schemes were implemented. Medical care facilities were facilitated.

An interesting example of the degree of complexity that can be found in such programs was the shelter project operated at Demra by the Irish and British voluntary groups: CONCERN and OXFAM. Using funds provided by OXFAM, CONCERN instituted a pilot project to find the best design for a low-cost housing unit. It had to be weather

resistant and socially acceptable to the population without
exceeding the inherently tight financial constraints.   Once
the design was agreed, CONCERN provided engineering
supervision and overall management of the house-building
scheme which followed.   OXFAM financed the initial 1,000 of
these housing units, while World Vision underwrote the cost
of the next 2,000 units.   The remaining 1,740 were provided
by further OXFAM grants.

Should the NGO involvement have been restricted to
short-term relief operations, leaving the long-term improvements to the government?   The Tongi situation gives some
idea of what might have happened had the NGOs restricted
their activities to the short-term.   In Table 7 we noted that
Government was committed to providing various medical
facilities.   In the end, however, they came not from Government but from Christian Health Services Bangladesh.
Sanitation arrangements were provided not by Government
but by OXFAM.   Although education facilities were obviously
considered a part of Government's activity, in the end they
were provided by the Salvation Army, Terres-des-Hommes
and Christian Health Services.   As can be seen in Table 9,
a similar situation evolved at the other resettlement camps
and a comparison of Tables 7 and 9 is instructive.

Although it is fully recognized that the NGOs moved in
to provide services because the Government of Bangladesh
failed to do so, at the same time one could argue in the
reverse.   Because the NGOs were willing to provide the
basic needs of the population of the resettlement camps, the
government was excused from its fundamental responsibilities
and commitments.   After all, it was not the NGOs who
forcibly removed the squatters from the cities but the
Government.   Therefore, a strong case could be made that it
was the Government's responsibility to provide these
services.

SUBSEQUENT DEVELOPMENTS AT TONGI AND DEMRA

As time passed, conditions at two of the three resettlement camps, Tongi and Demra, improved significantly.
Evidence of the actual improvement of circumstances at the
camps can be traced to as early as January 1976 when
journalists "followed up" on their horror stories of a year
before (The Guardian, 1976).   With the end of the 1975

monsoon and the drying out of the camps, the health situation became better. Even at Bashantek it was reported that the hospital facilities were finally being used for acute illnesses rather than merely for malnutrition. There was still some unease at Demra because of a persistent measles epidemic that appeared to have begun almost at the same time as the initial move. A house-building program was underway in Demra and certain Government work programs, such as road building, were being carried out with payment for labor being made in food.

The situation at Tongi provides a relatively good basis for comparisons with the situation there in earlier years. Six years after the camp was established, the Tongi site was beginning to look increasingly like a very large Bangladesh village. Most of the spine road that wound through the village was an all-weather one made of brick. The residents and the Government had reached a sort of agreement on leaseholds for the land on which the houses were situated. An annual rent of Tk. 1 (at a time when US \$1 = Tk. 15) was charged for each plot but interestingly, and perhaps ominously, the Ministry of Public Works continued to maintain overall control of the site by stipulating that, notwithstanding the lease, it could move anyone or everyone off the site with no more than a seven day notice. This seems to give some justification to the fears of one resident of the community who was interviewed by Khan (1979, p. 46), "the government has brought us here to clear the mess at this site and when it needs to develop another site which is a jungle it will relocate us again".

All housing materials at the site were a gift from various NGOs. Hommes-des-Terres and the Salvation Army house-building programs had provided material for 3,000 of these 9 foot by 18 foot bamboo frame and matting huts which accommodated up to ten people each. In 1979, a storm occurred which destroyed about 100 houses but these had been reconstructed by the agencies. Daily maintenance of the houses was strictly the responsibility of the householder.

The employment situation was still considered to be a major problem. Very few of the former squatters qualified to work at the local industrial estate. Most men in the camp travelled to Dhaka for two month stretches and then returned to Tongi to visit their families for a short holiday.

Table 9. Non Government Organization Activity in Resettlement Camps, 1975–1978.

Organization	Date started	Activities	Resources	Number served	Location of activity
Bangladesh Rural Advancement Committee (BRAC)		Community work			Mirpur
Terres-des-Hommes International Federation	1975	Feeding Children		About 3,000	Tongi
Church of Bangladesh (re-named Christian Health Services Bangladesh)	1975	Running a medical center with free medical facilities, also provision of a limited family planning program			Tongi
Salvation Army and Terres-des-Hommes	1975	Reconstruction of large number of thatches and three schools		School containing 1,200 students	Tongi
OXFAM and CONCERN	1975	Construction of public lavatories	53 units	35,000 in Demra 24,000 in Tongi 10,000 in Bashantek	24 units in Demra 18 units in Tongi 11 units in Mirpur

Organization	Date	Activity	Units	Beneficiaries	Location
OXFAM and CONCERN	1975	CONCERN launched shelter program funded by OXFAM	4,740 units		Demra
Bangladesh Volunteer Service (BVS)	June–July 1975	Formal education up to class 5 and job-oriented vocational training	Primary and vocational school, 1 orphanage for 50 children	Primary schools for 10,000 and vocational schools for 9,000	Demra and Mirpur
CONCERN and World Vision	1975	Construction of houses		About 35,000 people	Demra
CONCERN	1975	Construction of houses		About 10,000 people	Mirpur
CONCERN (and from 1976 to April 1977 with BVS)	1975–1977	Feeding program		4,500–8,000	Demra, Mirpur
Church of Bangladesh and Seventh-Day Adventist Janakalyan Sangstha	1975	Feeding program			Tongi
Church of Bangladesh	1975	House repairing			Tongi

Table 9. (continued)

Organization	Date started	Activities	Resources	Number served	Location of activity
Terres–des–Hommes	1975	Vocational training		125 people	Tongi
Church of Bangladesh	1975	Vocational training		25 trainees	Tongi
South American Baptist Mission, Terres–des–Hommes, Salvation Army	March 1976	Earthwork projects		2,520 laborers	Tongi
Islamia Mission	October 1978	Primary education to class 5 and religious education	1 school	About 300 students	Demra

Source: Khan (1979, Ch. 4).

Virtually none of the residents felt they could commute to Dhaka on a daily basis.

The Dutch section of Hommes-des-Terres ran two five-year schools at the camp which had a total enrollment of 2,000. They provided not only an education but a daily meal. These operated on morning and afternoon shifts. By the fifth year, enrollment had declined to twenty pupils. The nearest secondary school was in Tongi city and about twelve pupils attended it each year from the camp.

All schools in the resettlement camp were operated by the NGOs. In 1979, a minister of the Government had visited the camp and had declared an allocation of Taka 200,000 (about US $13,333) for the construction of a state school. The walls were completed when the money evaporated. Residents cynically suggested that if they could arrange another ministerial visit they could probably complete the building. Yet under Bangladesh law, even if it were completed, it would be necessary to operate it for one year with local funds before the government would provide grants for teachers to run it.

Vocational training was an important activity in the Tongi community. Two community centers ran courses for 200 women to teach them how to sign their names, to read Bengali and English. Perhaps of even greater relevance was the skill training center run by Hommes-des-Terres. Training was given on the center's fifteen handlooms, which were made in the carpentry training program. Thirty-two week courses were also given in jute handicrafts (the output going to local shops oriented towards foreign buyers), bicycle and rickshaw repair, tailoring and basket making.

By 1980, 60 young men had graduated from the carpentry training course which not only provided looms for the weaving classes but also desks and chairs for the school rooms. Upon completion of the course, they were awarded a fully equipped tool box. Of the graduates, 40 were reported to be working full-time, 10 worked three or four days per week while the remaining 10 had sold their boxes.

Most of the camp's activities and facilities were still provided by NGOs. Although in each of the resettlement camps, the Government appointed an administrator who was advised by a local committee, education, sanitation, housing

and a substantial proportion of employment was provided by
the charities. The water supply was provided by Government, yet the residents complained about non-existent
maintenance. If the pumps broke down, they remained
broken down.

What we see then are two camps that are poorly located
with respect to the types of employment that their residents
could expect to obtain. Because they were so far from
Dhaka, wage earners needed to stay away from their families
for extended periods of time. There was some evidence
that, as a result of such domestic instability, families had
broken up.

The improvements that had taken place in the Tongi
camp and in Demra, were largely the result of a permanent
location for the camps and a high degree of dedication and
imagination on the part of the international NGOs. The
investments that had been made by the charities, although
relatively modest in size, gave an air of stability and an
appearance of permanence to the two camps.

At the same time, however, one cannot help but wonder
whether this appearance of permanence was deceptive. As
we have seen, under existing lease arrangements with the
Ministry of Public Works, Tongi residents can be cleared
from the site on seven days notice. The situation at Demra
is perhaps even less secure. In May 1982, the Dhaka Water
and Sewerage Authority was involved in legal actions to
recover portions of that site from "illegal occupation" in
order to use it for the originally intended treatment plant
(Bangladesh Times, 1982).

CONCLUSIONS

This chapter has reviewed the rather subtle political
shifts that occurred after Independence in 1971 and how
these shifts affected the squatter population in the
Bangladesh cities. The root causes of the changing political
situation were due to a number of factors: the organizations
of society, the power of the bureaucracy, poverty and
foreign relations. Although none of these were directly
associated with the squatters, they became the scapegoat
when their removal was ordered.

Once the decision was made to clear Dhaka of its squatter population, events moved very quickly. The decision to resettle the squatters at the end of 1974 was probably only possible because of the relatively small number of squatters that existed. In other cities of the Third World, where the number of squatters may exceed the number of non-squatters, such a decision is not a feasible one. In such situations it is only where the land they occupy is required for other uses that resettlement on a partial basis is an option open to government. Even in Bangladesh, given the problems that emerged from the resettlement camps, such a partial solution concerning only land that was required for projects for which resources were available, would undoubtedly have been the better solution. Yet in Bangladesh, unauthorized settlement became tangled up with other issues which were totally unrelated to low-income groups within the capital city.

With their removal, abrupt though it may have been, the planning carried out to support it was inadequate. No effort was made to involve the squatters themselves in the solution. Instead, the removal was executed as a military operation. When the squatters arrived at the camps, they discovered that there was insufficient provision of services but also that the entire problem of their economic livelihood seemed to either have been overlooked or underestimated.

Without the active intervention of various NGOs at the Demra and Tongi resettlement camps, a more serious disaster might have resulted. Despite criticism by government officials, without their intervention the prospect of wide-spread starvation and more serious malnutrition was a very real one. As it was, these organizations, through their idealistic enthusiasm, allowed the Government to abdicate on a number of its inherent civic responsibilities. As a result, even the establishment of the camps at Demra and Tongi did not provide the Government with the necessary experience to develop new settlements of this type. The third camp at Mirpur will provide evidence by which this last statement can be tested, and it is to that experience that we now turn.

5. Toward a Permanent Solution at Mirpur

Officials in the Bangladesh Government seem to have considered the squatter resettlement camp at Bashantek in Mirpur to have been quite different from those at Demra and Tongi almost from the moment of its establishment. As a result of the problems already noted, the temporary settlement at Bashantek and its planned replacement in Mirpur received far more attention over the period from 1975 to 1981 than either of the other two camps. Much of this attention was from beyond the borders of Bangladesh. This case clearly illustrates the problems and misunderstandings that can arise not only through the more routine aspects of a major resettlement project but also those that can arise through the channels of international assistance.

In addition, the development of the squatter resettlement site in Mirpur throws light on certain major issues that can arise in the field of development planning, particularly planning for objectives which are primarily humanitarian and are sometimes encompassed by economists in that rather unfortunate phrase as "non-productive" investments. The project can be used to identify various constraints upon the project implementation process. In any project as complex as that planned for Mirpur, various impediments are bound to arise. Because of the prospect of difficulties with determining appropriate technology, securing adequate finance, preparing a proper organizational framework and making certain that all parties have the will to make the project a success, it would seem essential that account of such constraints be explicitly made in the planning process.

BASHANTEK: THE EARLY DAYS

Beginning on 4th January 1975, 3,044 families were deposited at an 88 acre unimproved site in the Bashantek area of Mirpur to the northwest of Dhaka. Like the resettlement schemes at Demra and Tongi, conditions were extremely difficult for those dispossessed from their squatter homes. There was, however, one significant distinguishing feature which differentiated the situation at Demra and Tongi on the one hand from that at Bashantek on the other. Within three years, with the aid of outside sources and some very hard work by the inhabitants, improvements were made transforming Demra and Tongi from temporary resettlement camps into permanent villages. At Bashantek, no such changes took place because of its supposed short life expectancy.

This temporary nature of the Bashantek settlement is an important variable in the present analysis. From the beginning of the program, a resettlement site had been planned for somewhere in the Mirpur area. Although from a geographical point-of-view, with a subsequent effect upon employment potential, Mirpur may be considered peripheral to Dhaka, from the viewpoint of Government, it was a natural location. A significant proportion of Bangladesh's refugee housing program had been centered in Mirpur. Furthermore, the land under Government control, albeit military control, lies primarily to the north of Dhaka, between the capital city and Mirpur. In view of this, it is not surprising that when the squatters were removed from Dhaka, a location in the Mirpur area became one of the three major reception areas. What could not be foreseen was the impact that this degree of temporariness would have upon the ultimate development of the new settlement.

In the early years, the similarities among the three sites were remarkably close. The horror stories that were so plentiful with respect to the situation at Demra and Tongi were heard in Bashantek as well. At the time of its establishment in 1975, there were no access roads to the settlement and as a result, the inhabitants were virtual prisoners. This was particularly true when it was discovered during the monsoon season of that year that the site, and area around it, were all subject to extensive flooding.

One of the NGOs involved in relief work at the site, OXFAM, became so concerned about the graphic reports of extreme poverty in the camps that they sponsored Dr Graeme Clugston, an Australian physician and nutritionist, to undertake a nutritional evaluation of the situation in the camps (OXFAM, 1978). It was reported (Finucane, 1978) that the conditions at Bashantek were the worst recorded anywhere within the region in over a quarter of a century. The combined results from Bashantek and Demra revealed that over 50% of the children within the age group one to four were moderately to severely malnourished.

As at the other camps, survival at the Bashantek resettlement colony was due largely to the active intervention of the NGOs. The squatters had been given a site that, although strictly speaking was located on government land, was on land which the Government had never really used. When, during the War of Liberation, village houses had been destroyed in the Bashantek area, rebuilding assistance had been offered by CONCERN, the Irish voluntary organization. As a result of this, local residents looked to CONCERN for further help in 1975. Although the relations between the transplanted squatters and the residents were strained since one group was now living on what was once the farmland of the other, the newcomers looked to CONCERN for help as well.

As it turned out, CONCERN was in a position to offer assistance. Working closely together, CONCERN and OXFAM started a feeding program at Bashantek using United Nations World Food Program provisions. A key element of the feeding program was the establishment of intensive care centers for the severely malnourished children identified in the OXFAM nutritional survey. This included feeding a small number of the more adversely affected children every four hours, even using intravenous and tube feeding where necessary. At the less critical level, two meals per day were provided for 11,200 settlement women and for 1,350 children.

OXFAM and CONCERN viewed their contributions at Bashantek as passing through three identifiable stages, from "emergency" to "relief" to "rehabilitation". In January 1976, the intensive care centers at Bashantek were closed indicating the improvements that had taken place and a progression along the sequence from emergency to rehabilitation.

Emphasis was then shifted to a more general feeding program and the provision of meals that could be linked with school activities.

A central part of CONCERN's program at Bashantek was a work program designed to aid 700 of the settlement's women. Based on the food for work principle, jute and cane materials were purchased and then transformed into finished products for sale in the local market. The women themselves were also involved in the feeding program and in return for their contributions to food preparation, received a daily wage of about four pounds of wheat per day.

Even these efforts, successful though they were in providing a very basic level of survival, were incapable of achieving more than this. Thus, one report described the situation in July 1977 as follows (OXFAM, 1978):

"Bashantek is still a miserable ghetto in every sense of the word. Basic shelters that were provided in January 1976 to hold the residents over until a resettlement site could be quickly designated, surveyed and officiated, have long outrun their intended life. Sanitation units and tubewells have served the camp well in providing an environmental buffer against infection and disease. However, the numbers of each are inadequate to serve a permanent community. Because resettlement to a new location had consistently been right on the "horizon" the number of these facilities had deliberately been kept to a minimum."

So we see that after two and one-half years, Bashantek was still considered to be very much of a temporary settlement. As a result, investment in infrastructure was not considered to be justified because of the imminent transfer of the inhabitants to a permanent location in Mirpur. At this stage, let us shift geographic locations from the temporary resettlement camp at Bashantek with all of its accompanying problems to the planning that was underway on the permanent settlement. As we will see, from the very beginning, outside assistance of an even more significant nature than that offered by the NGOs was expected at the new location.

FORMULATING THE MIRPUR SCHEME

The permanent site of the Mirpur settlement was to be located adjacent to the eastern boundary of Mirpur Municipality. The Government of Bangladesh was of the opinion that this was one area where the United Nations might justifiably become involved in offering assistance and in effect, helping to put into practice certain of the suggestions that had been incorporated in the 1974 report of the United Nations Mission on Urban Squatters.

This is not to suggest that the United Nations was unaware of the problems that had arisen in the development of the resettlement camps as it had been suggested that United Nations financial aid amounting to US $336,000 might be available to the Tongi settlement as early as 1976. Negotiations for this assistance floundered, however, with respect to one crucial point. The United Nations set as a prerequisite for assistance at Tongi the commitment by the Government that all participants be granted security of tenure for their plots at the site. The Government was unwilling to make such a commitment (UNCDF, 1977, p. 2).

The provision of financial aid from the United Nations for assistance to projects of this type is a somewhat complex affair and to fully understand the complications that eventually materialized, an understanding of the procedure itself is necessary. In 1977, the United Nations agency responsible for urban housing problems was the United Nations Center for Housing, Building and Planning[1]. The Center was a non-executing agency of the United Nations and as a result could not allocate funds of its own to its projects. The primary executing agency is the United Nations Development Program (UNDP) which has a worldwide network of technical assistance offices in over 100 Third World nations. Small projects, such as that proposed for assistance at Tongi and later for Mirpur are treated somewhat differently due to the high proportion of overhead to total costs that would inevitably result from such low-budget programs as these. For these projects, the United Nations Capital Development Fund (UNCDF) was suggested as a source of financial support.

The UNCDF was created in 1966 specifically to undertake financial commitments to projects of less than US $2 million. Although initially allocated no more than token funds, in 1973, the Fund was given enhanced status by the United Nations General Assembly and charged with providing capital financing to small projects in the least developed countries, such as Bangladesh. Specifically, the Fund was viewed as a granting agency of last resort for projects for which other sources of finance were not available either because they lacked bankable collateral or where credit-worthiness could not be established. Furthermore, no project is considered for funding by UNCDF unless it will directly and demonstrably help the genuinely poor.

A major advantage of using the Fund for such projects was that UN overheads could be kept to a minimum since the required technical assistance and administration of UNCDF projects is linked to existing personnel already in a country on other UNDP projects. In the case of Bangladesh, a UNDP-sponsored project on urban housing policies and programs already existed to which such linkages could be made. Obviously, then, UNCDF was the logical source of financing for a project of this type.

Another constraint that appears to have been important to the UNCDF, as interpreted by planners at the Center for Housing, Building and Planning, was some commitment to the continual improvement of such schemes. For example, rudimentary Government plans existed to rehouse the Banshantek squatters at a 40 acre settlement on the east side of Mirpur on undeveloped land. This scheme included the provision of one tubewell for each 50 families and one trench latrine for each 20 families. There was, however, no provision for either social or economic development. The Government planners had estimated the total cost of the project to be roughly the equivalent of US $775,000. In part because of the temporary nature of the proposed settlement, it was considered to be inappropriate as a project for UNCDF involvement. A possible additional reason for United Nations rejection of the plan might also have been the monsoon flooding danger to the site that had been allocated by the Government.

Realizing that United Nations assistance for the Mirpur project would not be forthcoming unless changes were made in the existing plans, the Government planners adjusted their own thinking. In effect, these adjustments reflected a shift from a commitment to a crude, rudimentary plan to ideas of a far more sophisticated nature. Not only did the

Government express agreement to the principle of security of tenure but also a commitment to the progressive improvement of the settlers' social and economic conditions. Even the problem of solving the potential flooding problems at the site became important. The United Nations Center for Housing, Building and Planning responded by sending a technical adviser to Dhaka in March 1977 to negotiate UNCDF involvement in the project.

The sudden importance given by Government officials to overcoming the flooding problem at the Mirpur site is significant. The plan agreed between the United Nations and the Government of Bangladesh was to expand the size of the settlement from 40 to 60 acres and to raise it by filling to above flood level, transforming it at the same time from a temporary camp to a more permanent settlement. The actual filling had begun in February, prior to the arrival of the technical adviser and was financed from the normal budgetary allocation of the Bangladesh Ministry of Public Works.

The topography of the site itself was, in fact, not only the major element of cost to be included in the scheme, but was to continue to influence and impede the solution to the resettlement program in future years. The site selected by the Government was adjacent to Sections IX, XI and XII of the established urban area of Mirpur, the numbered residential areas running from south to north along the community's eastern border. As one moves east from Mirpur, flood-free elevations give way to land which gently slopes downward to the Turag River. These lands, which were devoted to rice production, were subject to monsoon flooding.

The system for expressing elevations in Bangladesh, and hence for predicting the incidence and likelihood of flood, is complex. Public Works Data (PWD) is the official sea-level in Bangladesh and is used to quantify flood levels. Unfortunately, ordnance surveys are expressed in terms of Mean Sea Level (MSL) in Karachi, a reflection of pre-Independence history. PWD is 1 foot 6 inches higher than MSL.

To gain some idea of the effect of the topography upon the site, one need only note that the initial housing constructed at Mirpur Section XI was 28 to 38 feet PWD. At the eastern edge of that section, elevations were only about

6 feet PWD and the elevation drops further as one moves eastward across the proposed resettlement site. Based on annual records for 1953 to 1968 at Mirpur bridge, two miles to the south of the site, it is estimated that a flood of 27.2 feet PWD would cover the location once in twenty years (UNCDF, 1978, p. 21). Consequently, before the site could be used for a residential community, a solution to the flood problem had to be found.

The initial proposal from Government, even prior to the arrival of the United Nations Mission in March 1977, was to fill the site to 20.5 feet PWD, an elevation that would have prevented flooding in no more than 3 of the 16 years for which data were available. As 12 acres had already been raised to this level by March 1977, it was estimated that another 28 million cubic feet of earth was required to raise the remaining 51 acres to this minimal level. To raise the entire site to above the level required to completely eliminate the flood threat would require an additional 8 million cubic feet of fill. The total cost of such an operation would be Tk. 21,600,000 (US $1,440,000), a figure that was considered to be too high to be met by Government alone, hence the more modest, yet more vulnerable, solution.

By March 1977, when meetings took place between representatives of the United Nations and the Government, the 60 acre site was seen as adequate to house 2,300 families. Each family was to be allocated a plot of about 475 square feet, a basic one-room shelter, access to public utilities and community facilities. The facilities themselves were to be constructed with local labor. A major innovative idea in the plan was to establish a community savings and loan association which could make money available for the purchase of building materials (UNCDF, 1977, p. 3).

The housing units were to be patterned after houses developed by CONCERN for construction previously in the northern Bangladesh city of Mymensingh. When the displaced squatters had first arrived in Bashantek, the voluntary organizations, taking into account the poverty-stricken state of the community, donated for their use house construction materials of bamboo and polythene roofing materials. Within two years, these materials were already in a dilapidated condition. For a permanent settlement, more hardy materials were required and the Mymensingh-style house seemed to fit that need.

As envisaged for Mirpur, this consisted of a one room unit 12 feet by 10 feet. Ten 4-inch square reinforced concrete posts 10 and 12 feet long were to be placed in parallel rows to support rafters and timber purlins which held up a mono-pitch roof structure of corrugated iron sheets. The slope of the roof was designed to displace rain water onto a paved footpath between the units. The rafters themselves were held in place by reinforcing rods which extended beyond the end of the concrete pillars. Wall cladding consisted of bamboo mats which were secured by wire to the concrete posts (UNCDF, 1978). By improving the foundations, earthen floors and rain drainage, it was estimated that the life of such a structure might be 25 to 30 years. To reduce land consumption, the houses were to be built in semi-detached style, with a double bamboo matting between units to provide privacy.

The finance for the development of the scheme was to be shared by the UNCDF and the Government of Bangladesh. UNCDF was to pay foreign exchange costs of all imported items, including parts of the water supply system, part of the expense of the tubewell, plastic pipe, drainage pipes, overhead water pumps, the cost of concrete and steel for the house construction program and part of the sanitation and electricity expense. Additionally, UNCDF was to help finance the proposed community savings and loan society which would assist in the purchase of housing materials and to provide loans for potential entrepreneurs. The total UNCDF expense was agreed at $573,000 which comprised about one-half the total project cost excluding land. The Government of Bangladesh undertook to finance the remainder, which, in addition to land costs, included site preparation, the cost of indigenous house construction materials and the expense for the provision of most utilities other than drinking water which was made under a grant from UNCDF to the Dhaka Water and Sewerage Authority (UNCDF, 1977, p. 16).

The major element of site development cost in the scheme consisted of the house construction program. It was estimated that the two-family basic Mymensingh house could be constructed for Tk. 3,350. Sanitation for such a twin unit would add about Tk. 500, giving a total cost per double house of Tk. 3,850 or Tk. 1,925 ($129) on a per family basis. With the improvements upon the basic prototype that emerged from the negotiations between UNCDF and Government, the expected cost was to be Tk. 2,250 ($150). As 2,300 units were to be constructed, the result was a total housing cost of Tk. 5,175,000 ($345,000).

Three levels of participation were proposed in the implementation of the scheme with the Ministry of Planning responsible for overall coordination. The Government agreed to primary responsibility, with the implementing body being the Housing and Settlements Directorate of the Ministry of Public Works for site preparation, roads, the distribution of public utilities and plot partition.

The United Nations, through UNDP, was to provide technical assistance through existing programs in Bangladesh. In addition, the United Nations agreed to provide the short-term services of two consultants exclusively for the project. These included a planning and design consultant to cooperate with the Government for the establishment of appropriate design standards and the preparation of the necessary drawings and planning specifications for the project, and a financial analyst to review the budgetary and cost aspects of the resettlement exercise, to work with the Government in determining leasehold arrangements and to establish the feasibility of financing the amenities proposed for the project given the income of the inhabitants.

The final element of the implementation process involved the international NGOs. CONCERN was charged with implementing the site development component of the scheme, acting as contractor for the Government. OXFAM agreed to finance an economic and employment survey of the former squatters in an attempt to identify appropriate activities for inclusion into the scheme.

THE DETAILED PLANNING STAGE

The first of the two United Nations consultants to the Mirpur resettlement project arrived in September 1977. Over the next four months, the plans for the settlement changed significantly into a scheme that was far more complex than had been proposed previously.

Although originally it had been suggested that the monsoon flooding problem be overcome by filling the site to above flood level, the consultants proposed, and the Government accepted, that an enlarged site of 87 acres, be enclosed by an embankment (UNCDF, 1978, Annex 4).

The arguments in favor of an embankment rather than filling were primarily based on cost calculations. As already noted, the cost of filling the 60 acre site to above High Flood Level amounted to $1,440,000. Alternatively, the cost of an earthen dike, even if soil were brought in from outside the project, was estimated to be only $360,000. As at least part of the soil could be obtained locally by levelling the protected area to "polder-level", including that 12 acres of the site already raised to 20.5 feet PWD, it was expected that the actual cost would be considerably lower.

An additional disadvantage of the land-fill alternative was that even once it was completed and even if it was mechanically compacted, some subsidence would inevitably occur for at least one year. The likely result of the first monsoon rains would be to turn the area into a marsh. As a target date for completion by the monsoon period of 1978 was emerging, obviously this was an undesirable alternative.

Figure 7 gives the suggested location of the embankment with respect to Mirpur Municipality. The declines in elevation (expressed here in the older MSL terms) as one moves from west to east are significant, dropping from MSL 30.7 (32.3 feet PWD) at points immediately to the west of the proposed settlement to elevations as low as MSL 5.0 (6.6 feet PWD) along much of the eastern side of the site adjacent to the tributary to the River Turag.

Along the western side of the project location no embankment was required as the high land of residential Mirpur provided natural protection along that side. In fact, the drop in elevation along that line is abrupt and significant, forming a natural dividing boundary between land which is and land which is not flooded by the monsoon waters.

The polder-protected area was to contain the new community. The UNCDF consultant suggested a relatively formal layout for the settlement, a somewhat simplified diagram of which is included here as Figure 8. Parallel main roads, with a 75 foot right-of-way, diagonally divided the site with an area between them being devoted to a bazaar

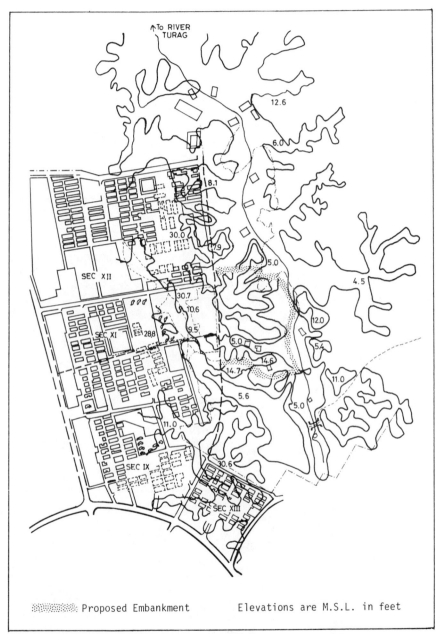

Fig. 7.   Embankment with Respect to Mirpur.

area, community buildings and open space. The main road followed the route of an existing high-tension electricity line which transversed the site, a factor which greatly reduced the cost of providing street lighting and other necessary electricity infrastructure. Secondary brick-paved roads, capable of vehicular use, perpendicular to the main roads were planned with staggered T-junctions to minimize congestion of the main road. The planned circulation system also included primary footpaths. Although some of these utilized the embankment, others ran parallel to the main roads among the housing areas.

As it was expected that much of the commercial activity of the community would be carried out within the housing areas, a relatively small area of land for single-purpose, commercial use was provided. Certain plots at either end of the main roads were designated for the community center, schools and training centers, the bazaar, workshops and a mosque. To provide accessibility for materials, the workshop area was placed adjacent to the existing built-up area of Mirpur Sector XI by a planned bus-stop on the existing roadway and near the point of vehicular access to the project area. Eight sites within the housing areas, each of 2,500 square feet, were reserved for kindergartens and Koranic schools.

It was proposed that the community buildings be constructed in a similar manner to the housing units. The concrete posts, corrugated iron roofing and bamboo wall matting could be designed to allow for the modular construction of such buildings, allowing a potential for future expansion if the need arose. If economic conditions improved for the community then permanent buildings could eventually be constructed to replace the initial, more temporary structures.

Provision was also included in the plan for open space and recreation areas. Not only was it anticipated that the embankment itself, with a design gradient of 1:2 would be used for this purpose, but a sports field was included on the south-eastern side of the site. Smaller green squares, 40 feet by 80 feet, were planned to separate the residential neighborhoods. These latter areas were multi-purpose, serving as sites for the local schools for younger children, play space, for grazing and for fish cultivation. These areas were also designed to provide space for sewerage

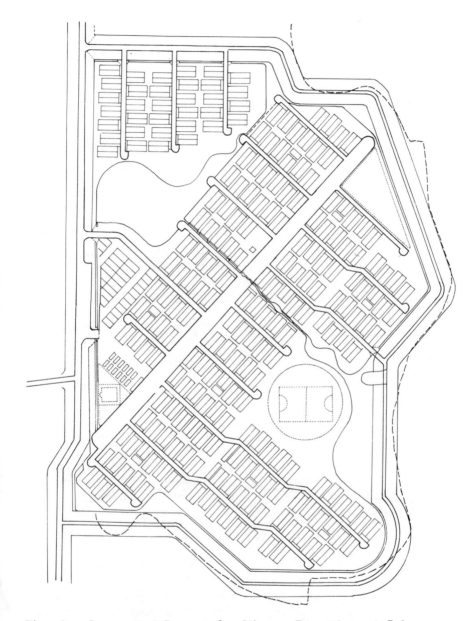

Fig. 8.   Suggested Layout for Mirpur Resettlement Scheme.
Source: Adapted from United Nations Capital Development
Fund (1978), Drawing B.

effluent pipes and treatment and, as a temporary measure during the first year of habitation, as sites for communal latrines and rubbish collection.

The principle of separation of fresh water supplies and sewerage effluent was followed closely. Whereas fresh water supplies were planned to serve the fronts of the houses along the secondary roads, sewerage effluent was confined to the back.

Water points were to be provided for each 16 housing units. These were to be located along the secondary roads with a set of three taps and a concrete base provided for each water point. As a public health measure, the water supply plans contained provision for the spatial separation of drinking water supplies, the washing of clothes and cooking areas. Given the arrangement of the water points, it would be unnecessary to carry water further than 28 yards to the furthest house in the group. Over the longer period, the plans included provision to add a 200,000 gallon overhead water tank to insure an uninterrupted supply of water.

The planning report was intentionally ambiguous concerning sanitation. It had been hoped that CONCERN's individual aqua-privies could be incorporated into each dwelling unit. A study of an 89 unit project previously constructed by CONCERN at Mymensingh which included the aqua-privy, revealed that due to social and technical problems, the latrines had been abandoned. It was hoped, however, that if instructions concerning their use could be offered and if assistance on maintenance matters could be provided, they would function adequately at Mirpur. It was proposed that a pilot test be carried out initially using the system on two neighborhoods, with six OXFAM emergency communal units serving the remainder of the community. The costing estimates provided by the consultants were based on the eventual provision of individual aqua-privies being provided for the entire project.

Concurrently, it was proposed that OXFAM undertake a Sanitation Management Program which would include a monitoring of problems that arose with respect to the individual toilet units, proposals for the treatment of a sewerage treatment system for the aqua-privy system and a consideration of the potential re-cycling for the production of bio-gas fertilizer and animal feeds.

One of the most serious problems facing such a polder-type area concerned storm drainage. It was recognized that without some kind of adequate drainage system, the entire area could easily become a muddy marsh, leading perhaps even to contamination of fresh water supplies from waste water. To prevent this, a far-higher standard of drainage system was proposed than that commonly found in such a low-income community environment.

Brick-lined channels with cement-rendering were suggested for location on either side of both primary and secondary roads. To prevent use being made of the drains for toilets, the consultants proposed that 3-inch thick reinforced concrete covers be used over all drains through residential neighborhoods. This was admitted to be a relatively expensive addition to the scheme as it required imported concrete and steel. Given what might be termed the luxury nature of the drain covers, it was proposed that the cost be covered by UNCDF.

The storm water would then be collected into a peripheral channel which would drain to a pumping station where it would be pumped over the embankment. In the assumption that there would be four inches of rain per day over the entire site during the peak monsoon period, it was concluded that a pumping requirement of 13 cubic feet per second (cu secs) was required. This was then augmented by 50% standby capacity, yielding a requirement of 20 cu secs.

Realizing the crucial aspects of such a pumping station, the consultants recommended the installation of six 4-cu secs pumps, three to be powered by diesel motors and the rest by electricity. It was suggested (UNCDF, 1978, p. 15) that adequate pumps were available in Bangladesh and that spare parts and the necessary knowledge of maintenance was readily available.

UNCDF'S FINANCIAL COMMITMENT TO THE PROJECT

A major task of the UNCDF consulting team was to estimate not only the total cost of the project, but the division of financial obligation between the two primary participants - the Government and the United Nations - and the proportion of those funds that might reasonably be

expected to be recouped from the future inhabitants through
rents and leases.   Although a considerably more detailed
look at the project's finances will be made later, it is
instructive at this stage to examine the figures suggested in
the course of the Mirpur settlement planning exercise.

The estimated costs of the project are shown in Table
10.   The total cost of the project, in 1977 prices, was
thought to be slightly in excess of Tk. 20 million
($1,334,788).   The source of finance, excluding land, was
roughly half from the Government of Bangladesh and half
from UNCDF.

The UNCDF team readily acknowledged that for a
low-income housing project directed at a target population
with a low-income generation ability, the plan was relatively
expensive.   One reason for the high cost was that shelter
was viewed as an integral part of the development scheme,
rather than being left to the residents, as is frequently
done in sites and services schemes.   It was suggested that
housing types to be built would have to be worked out in
collaboration with the Bashantek residents.   This was
particularly relevant if the Government were to insist on
repayment.

A survey of the Bashantek population carried out by
the Dhaka University Center for Urban Studies provided
socio-economic data upon which the project design was
based.   The consultants concluded that (UNCDF, 1978, p.
31) "considering average income of Tk. 310 per month, an
average household size of 4.8 persons and a share of food in
total expenditure which exceeds 80%, it can be assumed that
their propensity (to contribute toward the project) lies at no
more than 2-3% of income".   Although shelter cost of the
individual households was included in the grant to be
provided by UNCDF, the Ministry of Public Works was
interested in the possibility of recovering the cost of their
own investment in kind and infrastructure as the Government
did not feel it was in a position to subsidize the Mirpur
project on a permanent basis, or for that matter, any other
public housing project in the nation.

The consultants recognized the problems involved in
forcing the residents to make recurrent payments toward the
project yet realized that if no payments were expected, the

Table 10.   Mirpur Resettlement Project Costs (excluding land).

Item	Tk.	US	Per cent of total cost
Elements to be financed by the Ministry of Public Works:			
Embankment	5,490,000	366,000	27.4
Site grading	2,273,832	151,589	11.4
Pumps/pump station	1,300,000	86,667	6.5
Drainage	221,640	14,776	1.1
Sub-total	9,285,472	619,032	46.4
Elements financed by the United Nations Capital Development Fund:			
Drain covers	554,040	36,936	2.8
Water points	98,000	6,533	0.5
Sanitation	1,798,600	119,907	9.0
Street lighting	47,000	3,133	0.2
Shelter	3,797,300	253,153	19.0
Community facilities*	520,087	34,672	2.6
Financial management	158,950	10,597	0.8
Monitoring	45,000	3,000	0.2
Sub-total	7,018,977	467,931	35.1
Elements financed jointly by various agencies:			
Roads/footpaths (Ministry of Public Works and United Nations Capital Development Fund)	1,525,500	101,700	7.6
Water supply (Dhaka Water and Sewerage Authority and United Nations Capital Development Fund)	2,191,875	146,125	10.9
Sub-total	3,717,375	247,825	18.6
Total	Tk. 20,021,824	$1,334,788	100.0

*Excludes equipment, running costs and maintenance.
Source: UNCDF (1978).

housing units were likely to be rented out to other residents while those for whom they were intended squatted elsewhere, living off the rent proceeds. Therefore, it was proposed that rents be collected from residents on a neighborhood basis, giving considerable latitude to the application of moral pressure on those who withheld payment. Furthermore, it was suggested that bonuses of up to 10% of rental income might be granted to neighborhoods which succeeded in having no defaulters. To encourage collection, a proportion of the income might be made available to the neighborhoods themselves to spend as they wished on community development projects.

In the first instance, it was anticipated that a grant from the UNCDF would be used to provide financial management for the settlement. After a period of three years, the residents of the project itself would be expected to take over this responsibility.

An additional expense that had to be considered for collection from the residents was for ground rent. The standard charge for ground rent in Bangladesh at the time was Tk. 2.50 per 100 square yards. In terms of the plot sizes in the Mirpur project, this amounted to somewhat less than Tk. 1.00 per year. This too was to be collected on a neighborhood basis and paid collectively to the Land Revenue Account.

Full repayment of the Government's expenditures could only be expected to occur over the longer term. Therefore, it was suggested that after four or five years from occupancy, the Government should reconsider the question of the lease arrangement.

An integral part of the project, and one which differentiated it significantly from other more traditionally-oriented housing projects, was the emphasis given toward economic improvement. An employment generation survey was to be carried out by the voluntary associations involved in the project. Given the relatively high cost of the project and the low incomes of the target population, perhaps some effort was inevitable and necessary to improve the economic conditions of the inhabitants.

Certainly if the income did increase, then a part of it could justifiably be expected to repay the Ministry of Public

Works' expenditures and, at that time, the possibility of a 33 year lease should be seriously considered. In view of the Bashantek residents' desire for security of tenure in their living accommodation, this was highlighted by the consultants as an extremely important issue in the planning process.

Another finding of the socio-economic survey of Bashantek residents was that they placed a relatively low priority on housing aspirations and gave greater emphasis to employment possibilities. As a result of this the consultants suggested that when discussions were held with the future residents of the scheme, rather than merely labelling the project as a shelter scheme, emphasis should be placed upon the potential for (UNCDF, 1978, p. 26) "integrated development involving gradual upgrading of living standards and conditions, through collective and individual employment generation activities combined with community development efforts, continual improvement of shelter and community facilities as well as communal maintenance of infrastructure".

EVALUATING THE PLANNING EFFORT

Certain important points which would seem likely to have some effect upon the implementation of the project are already beginning to emerge from the case study material. For two years after the removal of the squatters from Dhaka the Government appears to have been either indecisive as to which course to pursue or indifferent as to the ultimate fate of the Bashantek residents. Although periodic negotiations had been carried on with the United Nations concerning possible assistance, it was not until the arrival of the UN technical adviser in March 1977 that the Government focused its efforts on a single location. We do not know whether the apparent change of heart was one that genuinely developed at that time within certain Government officials or whether it was one imposed by the strong personalities and apparent power possessed by those representing the United Nations.

In any event, as is so often the case, from March 1977 the planning process of the Mirpur Resettlement Scheme appears to have taken on a momentum of its own. Expatriate consultants were recruited and dispatched to Bangladesh. There they carried out their terms of reference and pre-

sented the Mirpur plan which was to be implemented by the
Government and to be partially financed by UNCDF. One
cannot help but wonder, however, whether the suggestions
made in the plan were appropriate to the Bangladesh
environment or whether they reflected an unbridged cultural
gap between the sophisticated planners from the United
Nations and a target population unaccustomed to such
advanced technology.

For example, use of relatively inexpensive, flood-prone
land protected by an embankment was an innovative idea
which assumed a high degree of technological sophistication
to carry it out successfully. Similarly, the provision of
actual custom-designed housing complete with flush toilets
was another innovative element of the plan. Although both
custom-designed housing and flush toilets had been already
tried out in a CONCERN-sponsored housing project in
Mymensingh, the toilets at least appear to have been an
unsuccessful inclusion.

The same can be said for elements of the drainage
system. The need for an efficient drainage system in such
an embankment-protected residential scheme is apparent.
Here too, fairly sophisticated levels of technology were
assumed although the pumps specified for the scheme should
have given a more-than-sufficient safety margin. The drain
covers, on the other hand, by Bangladesh traditions, border
on the luxurious, but then they were, in effect, a gift from
the United Nations.

Finally, the inclusion of a comprehensive sewerage
effluent collection network and a complete water distribution
system, of street lights and planned community buildings
were all largely unprecedented suggestions in the planning
of low-income housing within the Bangladesh environment.

Yet, as we have seen, the planners considered the
project to be somewhat more than merely a low-income
housing scheme. By including an employment generation
exercise within their report to improve the economic conditions of the inhabitants, it is apparent that the UNCDF
consultants were specifying a plan for a social experiment of
a very adventurous nature. Was it too adventurous? We
must defer seeking an answer to this question until we
consider the implementation of the Mirpur scheme in a later
chapter.

However, one can see already that certain difficulties might be expected to arise based strictly upon our review of the plan. For example, we have seen that UNCDF is exclusively a funding body. Although it can send out consultants to a project it does not operate through its own permanent project implementation staff. As a result, success in carrying out its schemes rests on the goodwill of the Government or on that of UNDP project staff already involved in related projects on behalf of the United Nations or on the goodwill of the international voluntary organizations whose personnel appear to have already had a significant influence on the planning of the project. Were the hopes of such necessary goodwill justified?

With respect to the attitude of the Government, the missing two years between the removal of the squatters in January 1975 and the new-found commitment to Mirpur in March 1977 might have been considered to be slightly worrying. Although the consultants' report legally bound no one to do anything, it is apparent that the so-called "project document", which we will be analyzing in the next section, would, when it was approved by all parties, organize a fairly large number of diverse governmental and non-government organizations to carry out their implementation tasks on the Mirpur project. Attitudes toward this document will no doubt give us an indicator about the probable success in implementing the scheme.

With respect to the United Nations personnel in Dhaka who might be able to "help out" with the project, there were many. The United Nations Development Program in Bangladesh is among the largest of UNDP offices in the Third World. At the time the Dhaka Mission was headed by an extremely able Resident Representative who in turn was assisted by a first-rate staff. Among the projects which were underway at that particular time were at least two which were fairly closely related. One was a National Physical Planning Project which included both a physical planning and a training component. The second project concerned Urban Housing Policies and Programs. Personnel from both projects became involved with the Mirpur scheme although it is only fair to note that those involved considered this to be of secondary importance to their primary roles in Bangladesh. As a consequence, their commitment to Mirpur was necessarily of a lower order than to their primary projects.

Goodwill was required on the part of the NGOs. In part, the commitment of these organizations flowed directly from past events. Because CONCERN had been associated with projects in the Bashantek area since 1972, they became involved in emergency relief operations when the squatters were moved there. And because they had worked with residents of the squatter resettlement camp from 1975 to 1978, they had a genuine interest in the development of the permanent camp. Similarly OXFAM, which was frequently associated with CONCERN in various activities, particularly it seems in the role of a banker, joined with them in attempting to improve the conditions of the former squatters.

There was, however, another voluntary organization that became increasingly associated with the project and its motives for involvement were slightly more complex. This was the Bangladesh Rural Advancement Committee (BRAC). Initially, the UNCDF team had foreseen BRAC's role to be associated with OXFAM in the employment generation survey.

BRAC was formed in 1972 as a relief group working with Hindu fishermen in the rural northeast of Bangladesh after the War of Liberation (Campbell, 1981). As the organization matured it became increasingly involved in development projects but worked almost entirely in rural areas. Unlike OXFAM and CONCERN, BRAC was an indigenous Bangladesh group, founded, and for that matter still run, by a small group of young people drawn from the educated middle and upper classes. Although it generates some of its own funds locally from the operation of a printing press, it is primarily dependent upon foreign donors and thus, not unexpectedly, on the Mirpur project, became associated with OXFAM.

BRAC's reason for becoming involved in the project was that although the Bashantek squatters had been urban residents, the entire scheme was consistent with its rural objectives[2]. It was readily acknowledged that voluntary organizations on their own could not succeed in projects of this type and required Government involvement. The projects constituted small pilot programs where feasibility tests on alternative approaches to urban housing, community and neighborhood concepts and employment creation strategies could be made prior to undertaking large scale urban development programs.

According to the BRAC argument, their own motivation toward involvement was dictated by the failures of other such programs. Failures which had occurred because: (1) there had been no attempt to study the characteristics of the community; (2) the organizing personnel did not speak Bengali; (3) no attempts were made to create responsible grass roots organizations; (4) there was no serious attempt at employment generation; (5) there was too great an emphasis on short run as against longer term efforts; and (6) no attention had been given at the design stage to realistic plans for maintenance. In hopes of overcoming these potential pitfalls and making a positive contribution, BRAC wished to participate.

Thus, what we have is a relatively modest program which by normal development project standards might even be labelled as inexpensive, but one which incorporated a fairly large number of potential innovations. This attempt at finding new ways of doing things even extended over into the groups and organizations that were involved. Although one would expect to find Government as a participant, the inclusion of international and indigenous voluntary organizations playing such an active role is rather unusual in United Nations projects of this type. The question in which we are now interested is how the project was implemented. We complete this chapter with a description of the legal document that was designed to guide participation and in the next chapter we begin to tackle the detailed questions associated with such efforts.

THE MIRPUR PROJECT DOCUMENT

In March 1978, the Mirpur resettlement plan received the approval of the United Nations and, as a result, UNDP acting on behalf of UNCDF, was in a position to draw up the project document which set out procedures and conditions for making the grant. This document actually consisted of two parts, a grant agreement and an administrative agreement. The former was to be signed by the Government and UNDP on behalf of UNCDF. The administrative agreement, which actually is the more interesting of the two, required approval by the Government, UNDP, BRAC, CONCERN and OXFAM.

The grant agreement itself consisted of a number of sections, or articles. Article I defined the total amount of UNCDF's contribution and specified how it should be disbursed. We find, for example, that the total of the grant had now increased to US $812,000 compared to a significantly lower amount in Table 10.

There were several reasons for this increase, none of which were really all that mysterious. In the cost calculations shown in Table 10, the cost of shared projects, such as roads/footpaths and the water supply, were presented in aggregated form. In the grant agreement, they were disaggregated showing the UNCDF's share of roads and footpaths was to be $55,000, while the foreign exchange element of the water supply system was $87,000. The contribution toward community facilities had been increased from $34,672 to $80,000, while the contribution to management facilities and monitoring was actually reduced from $13,597 to $7,000. The major change, however, was the inclusion of a 10% unallocated contingency category ($65,000) and an allowance for a 15% cost escalation ($97,500).

The remaining sections of the grant agreement were concerned with procedures to be followed. Article II specified that the organizations carrying out the implementation on behalf of the Government would perform their tasks efficiently. It specified how materials for the projects were to be purchased and the types of records that were to be kept.

Article III specified that the United Nations and Government should cooperate fully to meet the objectives of this project and that problems that arose with respect to the progress of the project should be fully discussed. Article IV was concerned with the suspension or termination of the grant if UNCDF should perceive any circumstances which might interfere with successful completion of the work.

Article V was devoted to the settlement of disputes between the two parties, including, if necessary, a provision for arbitration and even the ultimate involvement of the President of the International Court of Justice. In Article VI, we find a provision that the obligations under the grant would run for two years from the date of signature while Article VII was to contain the names and addresses of the persons designated by both sides to carry out action under the agreement.

The administrative agreement consisted of a short description of the project, virtually a one page summary of the UNCDF consultants' report, and most important of all, the implementation plan. In fact, as we will see in the following chapter, it was this document that led to a considerable amount of controversy with respect to carrying out the project and a review of the implementation plan is an essential prerequisite to our analysis of the implementation of the project.

The implementation plan identified seven participants and specified the tasks they were expected to undertake. The first of these was the Bangladesh Ministry of Public Works. The Ministry was expected to "construct the embankment and pump house, install the pumps, undertake the site grading and construct storm water drainage as well as main and secondary roads ..."[3]. In addition they were expected to survey and register the residential plots and finance the drainage pump operation for a period of three years. Maintenance of the embankment, drainage and road systems were also, in the first instance, an obligation of the Ministry.

The Dhaka Water and Sewerage Authority was to construct the deep tubewell and the water reticulation system. Whereas imported materials were to be paid for from the UNCDF grant, the cost of construction was to be borne by Government. Furthermore, the Authority was to undertake to operate and maintain these facilities.

Dhaka Electrical Supply was to supply, install and maintain the necessary electrical transformers and street lighting meters.

Among the NGOs, BRAC was to be responsible for community development, assistance to residents during the transition period, to supervise the site management office, to carry out the employment generation survey and to advise the elected neighborhood representatives on levels and collection of contributions toward the cost of housing. It is apparent that BRAC's role at Mirpur had grown very significantly since their association with the project.

OXFAM was again assigned the banker's role. They were expected to fund BRAC's community development team, a sanitation management program and the operating cost of the site management office for three years.

CONCERN was largely involved in subcontracting the construction of various elements of the UNCDF contribution. These included water points, drain covers, footpaths, shelter, community buildings, street lighting and the aqua-privies.

Finally, UNDP was, in addition to coordinating UNCDF inputs, responsible for arranging a short-term small industry consultant to assist on the employment generation survey, various technical follow-up missions and to arrange for the monitoring surveys of the project by the Center of Urban Studies at the University of Dhaka. In addition, UNDP assigned the project manager of the study on Housing Policies and Programs to assist a coordinating committee on the planning and implementational aspects of the UNCDF consultants' report.

CONCLUSION

This chapter has been concerned with the planning-related aspects of the Mirpur Squatter Resettlement Project. Two important elements emerge from the analysis. The first of these concerns the number of technologically-advanced innovations that were suggested by the plan. As the implementation of such a project will necessarily be dependent upon Bangladesh contractors, the likely success or failure of the project would seem to be closely related to their ability to cope with such new ideas in an environment which was not necessarily accustomed to such advances.

The star role as we will see in the chapter on implementation will be taken by one of the innovations: the embankment. The UNCDF consultants suggested a plan that was totally dependent upon the successful completion of this element. In fact, without it, no other part of the project could be completed due to the danger of monsoon flooding that existed at the site.

A careful reading of the information in the implementation plan in the draft project document reveals the second major element to emerge from this chapter. This concerns the coordination of the various organizations involved in implementing the project and the dedication of each of them to the overall project objective. Various constraints which might be expected to affect the implementation of the project have also been identified.

6. Financial Feasibility and the Planning Process

In recent years, increasing attention has been given to three key interrelated terms within the field of Third World housing finance: affordability, cost recovery and replicability. In operational terms, affordability means that project designers should view the cost of housing as a variable which should be reduced until it comes within the reach of the target population. Cost recovery means that the costs associated with such a project should be collected in the form of leases, rents or sales to the recipients. Replicability implies that the collected funds should be available to construct further projects to provide shelter for other target populations. As Prakash notes (1985, p. 1), "affordability is the key to cost recovery, and cost recovery is the key to replicability".

The Mirpur project design has now been set forth and it remains to be seen if such a plan meets these important criteria or not. For countries such as Bangladesh, where incomes are low even by Third World standards, this is a critical stage, for all kinds of decisions are required concerning subsidies, recovery levels and economies if the costs and revenues do not coincide. In turn, finance forms a major constraint upon the implementation of schemes such as the one proposed for Mirpur. In this chapter, the various issues related to the financial feasibility of the Mirpur Resettlement Project are considered. The first of these problems is to determine how much the plan proposed for the project really cost. This is frequently far more complicated than one might expect as the scope and design of all projects evolve over time and this in turn affects cost. Yet in order to determine whether or not the project was financially feasible, not only are the cost figures required but so too are another almost equally elusive set of numbers related to the rent paying ability of the settlement's residents.   This in turn depends on interest rates, repayment periods, ground rents, settlement sizes and future income projections. It is apparent that although some of these variables are within the control of the project planners, a number are determined by completely external factors.

Within the Mirpur context, incomes were so low that most of the target population for the project could not afford even the low-cost scheme that has been described.   Therefore, some thought is given in this chapter of seeking alternative ways of lowering project costs and, in this manner, increasing affordability.

ESTIMATING PROJECT COSTS

Attention has been directed toward the development of the ideas that were involved with the resettlement in Mirpur Section XI of the former squatters of Dhaka.   Anyone attempting to maintain a running total of how much this project changed in cost from its inception in 1975 until the beginning of the implementation phase in 1978 has seen a wide variation in the proposed costs.   Five distinct sets of project costs for the Mirpur Resettlement Project scheme can be identified over this relatively short period.   Admittedly, these are not necessarily estimated costs for the same project as there was, as we have seen, an evolutionary change in what was expected at the site.

The first identifiable project was the temporary "rehabilitation" scheme presented by the Ministry of Public Works and Urban Development in January 1975 (1975a) at the time of the initial clearing of the squatters from Dhaka. With 3,044 families located in Bashantek as of the end of January of that year, the estimated cost of emergency provision of water and sewerage facilities plus administrative buildings was Tk. 1,398,208 (US $173,690).

The second plan was presented almost simultaneously and provided estimated costs, compiled again by the Ministry of Public Works (1975b), for a permanent site and services scheme at Mirpur.   This particular scheme included the

purchase cost of 68 acres of land and was designed to
accommodate 2,003 families. Total estimated cost of the plan
was Tk. 88,022,623 ($10,934,487), which was, incidentally,
by far the most expensive scheme proposed for the Mirpur
area.

The third suggestion was a general scheme which was
referred to in the 1977 report prepared by the technical
adviser from the United Nations Center for Housing, Building and Planning (UNCDF, 1977, p. 6), stating that prior to
the arrival of that mission, the Government of Bangladesh
had been considering a 40 acre site and services scheme in
the Mirpur area at a cost of Tk. 11,625,000 ($775,000).

The fourth suggestion followed from that 1977 mission
and the idea of a permanent settlement on filled ground in
Mirpur Section XI. This plan was to accommodate 2,300
families on a 60 acre site at a total cost of approximately Tk.
34,831,890 ($2,322,126). This cost is no more than approxi-
mate as a finalized estimate of the total project cost apparently was never made. It should be recalled, however, that
in the UNCDF consultants' 1978 report (UNCDF, 1978, p. 2),
the cost of filling the site was estimated at $1,440,000 and
the cost of the embankment was set at $452,662. If one
takes the UNCDF consultants' total estimated project cost,
$1,334,788, subtracting the cost of the embankment and then
adding the cost of the land filling, the approximate figure
results. To some degree it is an overestimate in that it
involves a double counting of a proportion of the filling.
Beyond that, it assumes that the physical layout of the
settlement envisaged in the 1977 mission report is identical to
that suggested by the UNCDF consultants in 1978.

The fifth plan which was suggested, and the one with
the most documentation, was the polder-protected-settlement
proposed by the UNCDF consultants in 1978 (UNCDF, 1978).
The estimated cost of this 87 acre development for 2,300
families was Tk. 20,021,805 ($1,334,787) excluding the cost
of the land. If the land was valued at Tk. 45,000 per acre,
a figure used the following year in estimates by the Housing
and Settlement Directorate, then the total cost of the planning project would have been about Tk. 23,936,824
($1,595,788).

The figures given here are summarized in Table 11.

Table 11. Summary of Cost Estimates for Mirpur Resettlement Scheme.

Type of settlement	Year	Acreage	Number of households	Total cost
1. Ministry of Public Works estimate for temporary resettlement scheme	1975	–	3,044	Tk. 1,398,208 ($173,690)
2. Ministry of Public Works estimate for permanent resettlement plan	1975	68	2,003	Tk. 88,022,623 ($10,934,487)*
3. Government of Bangladesh scheme for Mirpur	about 1976	40	not determined	Tk. 11,625,000 ($775,000)
4. Plan resulting from UN Center for Housing, Building and Planning Mission for Mirpur Section XI	1977	60	2,300	Tk. 34,831,890 ($2,322,126)
5. Plan resulting from UNCDF Mission	1978	87	2,300	Tk. 23,936,824 ($1,595,788)

* The relevant rate of exchange in January 1975 was US $1.00 = Tk. 8.05. After April 1975 it is assumed to be constant at US $1.00 = Tk. 15.00.

THE PROBLEM OF FINANCIAL FEASIBILITY

At this stage, it is important to assess the financial feasibility of this final proposal for the Mirpur project. It has been argued in Chapter 1 that lack of resources constitutes a potentially major impediment upon implementation. If the project is found to be beyond the realm of feasibility, given the limited economic circumstances of the former squatters coupled with the cost of the project, then its successful implementation would be dependent upon the resource contributions of a Government which has already been seen to have limited financial means. If this is indeed found to be the case, one might have expected before implementation began that difficulties would inevitably arise and that other projects where the financial returns were more promising would be given higher priority by Government decision-makers. If the Mirpur project is found to be within this category of projects which require external subsidies, it would be likely that it would be relegated to a lower priority for implementation and that this in turn would adversely affect its successful completion.

In order to assess affordability, we are interested in comparing the costs of the 1978 UNCDF plan with the rent paying capacity of the project's target population, that is, the inhabitants of Bashantek. This analysis necessarily requires a number of simplifying assumptions, some of which may be considered to be of doubtful validity. Given the difficulty involved, in every instance the benefit of doubt will be given to the project. In other words, in this analysis it is deemed preferable to overestimate the rent paying capability of the inhabitants rather than to underestimate it, to underestimate expected interest charges rather than to overestimate them, to make the repayment period too long rather than too short, etc.

The initial problem facing such analysis is to determine which project costs would have to be recovered as this would necessarily form the basis of annual charges to the tenants of the settlement. Ample evidence exists to suggest that the Government of Bangladesh hoped to recover all of its own contribution to the project in the form of rental charges to the inhabitants. As the UNCDF report (1978, p. 30) notes, "any low-cost urban housing program must be conceived in terms of economic viability as the Government of Bangladesh cannot subsidize even a small share of the effective housing

demand".   At another point it is suggested that the Government had a desire to recover the costs of both land and
infrastructure, even if it was necessary to wait until the
income levels of the residents increased to such a point as
this was possible.

Two options on recovering costs seem to exist.   In the
first option, the Government would base rental charges upon
its own contribution to infrastructure, maintaining its
ownership over the land used by the project.   As early as
1973, this alternative was suggested by the United Nations
Mission on Urban Squatters (United Nations, 1973, p. 16) in
its consideration of the potentials to be derived by site and
services schemes in Bangladesh: "The land should remain the
property of the Government to prevent speculation or other
misuse.   Tenure should be granted, whether to individuals
or cooperatives, on a long-term lease at a reasonable ground
rent".   That report went even further (p. 17) in suggesting
that of infrastructural costs, the inhabitants should be
expected "to repay at least part of the capital expenditure
with interest".

On the basis of these statements, then, using 1978
project costs, it might be expected that the Government
could wish to recover as much as Tk. 10,870,500 ($724,700)
of the total expected project expenditure of Tk. 20,021,805
($1,334,787), the remainder being contributed on a gift basis
by UNCDF.   The major exclusion is, of course, the cost of
the 87 acres of land to be occupied by the project.

Rather than including the sale price of the land in the
total, rental charges based on a lease arrangement would
have been charged.   Although the Government had been
willing to agree to a 10-year lease on the land, an underlying factor that initially led to agreement on proceeding on
the project, the UNCDF mission argued strongly for a
33-year lease, a tenure period that would significantly
increase the likelihood of cost recovery, particularly when
coupled with the expected employment generation program.

As noted in the 1978 report, the standard charge for
ground rent in Bangladesh was Tk. 2.50 per 100 square
yards.   Given the plot sizes planned for the Mirpur project
this amounted to an annual charge of about Tk. 1.00 per
plot.

The second cost recovery option open to the Government might have been to sell the plots to the settlers, including in the price not only the infrastructural items in the rental bill but also the cost of the land. If the Housing and Settlements Directorate's 1979 assessment of this land was considered to be valid, that is that the land was worth Tk. 45,000 ($3,000) per acre, then the 87 acre tract would add Tk. 3,915,000 ($261,000) to the amount to be recovered. This total amount to be recovered then rises to Tk. 14,785,500 ($985,700).

Under such conditions, the length of the lease agreement obviously disappears only to be replaced by the length of the repayment period to be allowed. To maintain comparability with the necessary calculations that result from the option concerning the recovery of infrastructural costs alone, let us include two possible repayment periods in this analysis: 10 years and 33 years.

As in the case of the amount of costs to be recovered, several options also exist concerning the household population over which these costs should be spread. The population of the Bashantek settlement at the time of the 1978 UNCDF report was estimated to be 2,201 households. According to the project design documents, adequate land existed within the embankment for 3,500 households.

In the present calculations, two target populations are selected. The first is the original target of 2,300 households. The higher figure of 3,500 households is also analyzed to see what the effect would be of spreading the costs to be recovered over a larger number of families. Although the community sizes vary, it is assumed that the cost elements do not. Since it is Government costs that are to be recovered and since they were primarily for such infrastructural elements as the embankment, levelling of the site, roads, etc., items which are largely independent of the actual number of households in the community, the costs were assumed to be equal in both cases. Had there been a desire to recover UNCDF expenses, which were very closely related to the number of housing units in the settlement, then this assumption would have required considerable amendment. As it is, this assumption may underestimate the amount to be recovered and thus should result in higher affordability among the target population.

To this stage, six possibilities for the analysis of financial viability for the project exist: two options concerning cost recovery, two options concerning the time period for the recovery and two options on target populations.

The final variable to be included is the interest rate that might be charged on the capital expenditure. This, of course, merely adds to the costs which must in turn be recovered from the tenants. Here too, a number of alternative possibilities would seem to exist. The general rate for borrowing from the Bangladesh Bank from June 1975 through the relevant period to 1980 was 8%, which, because of its domestic applicability, seems to represent a reasonable figure for the present calculations. However, alternatives can also be examined such as the more restrictive rate of 12%, a subsidized rate of 5% (which is even slightly lower than the rate charged at that time on formal agricultural loans by the Bangladesh Samabaya Bank), or the ultimate in the provision of subsidies, an interest-free loan.

All of these per household cost items under the various assumptions examined are drawn together in Table 12. The upper part of the Table is based on an assumed target population for Mirpur of 2,300 households while the basis of the calculations in the lower part of the Table is 3,500 households. Interest at various rates is compounded over 10 and 33 years. The necessary payments when land is excluded includes a charge of Tk. 1.00 per year as leasehold payment. In Table 13, these data are presented on a community basis, where each element of the upper part of Table 12 is multiplied by the target population of 2,300 families and the lower elements of that Table by 3,500 families.

Once it is known how much must be paid annually the next problem is to examine the income distribution of the potential residents on a similar basis. The survey of the Bashantek residents by the University of Dhaka's Center for Urban Studies in conjunction with the UNCDF (1978, Annex 2) design scheme provides the basic data. Information was collected on the total monthly income per family. Such data must be interpreted with care as squatters in Bangladesh frequently understate their incomes on the expectation that the poorer they appear, the more likely the Government is to provide them with free facilities (United Nations, 1973, p. 8). Despite such shortcomings, income distribution estimates

Table 12. Annual Repayments Required per Household on Mirpur Resettlement Project under Varying Assumptions (1978 costs).

Interest rates	0%		5%		8%		12%	
Time period in years:	10	33	10	33	10	33	10	33
Target Population: 2,300 households								
Full repayment of infrastructure only including lease charge	Tk.474 ($32)	Tk.144 ($10)	Tk.613 ($41)	Tk.296 ($20)	Tk.705 ($47)	Tk.411 ($27)	Tk.837 ($56)	Tk.582 ($39)
Full payment of infrastructure	Tk.643 ($43)	Tk.195 ($13)	Tk.832 ($55)	Tk.402 ($27)	Tk.958 ($64)	Tk.558 ($37)	Tk.1,138 ($76)	Tk.790 ($53)
Target Population: 3,500 households								
Full repayment of infrastructure including lease charge	Tk.312 ($21)	Tk.95 ($6)	Tk.403 ($27)	Tk.195 ($13)	Tk.463 ($31)	Tk.271 ($18)	Tk.551 ($37)	Tk.383 ($26)
Full repayment of infrastructure and land	Tk.422 ($28)	Tk.128 ($9)	Tk.547 ($36)	Tk.264 ($18)	Tk.629 ($42)	Tk.367 ($24)	Tk.48 ($50)	Tk.519 ($35)

are obviously essential for analysis of this sort and as a result no option exists to using it in its present form.

The CUS survey sampled 201 of the 2,201 families in Bashantek. The resulting monthly data has been converted here to annual totals to conform with the annual basis used for the repayment calculations[1]. The total Bashantek household population is then distributed to income classifications on the basis of the survey results.

The most vital data for planning analysis were, unfortunately, not collected. This concerned the expenditure pattern which would have revealed what proportion of total family income was available for expenditure on housing. Certain expenditure surveys are made on a regular basis by the Bangladesh Bureau of Statistics of the Dhaka area. However, as these are for the middle class and for government employees, it is extremely unlikely that the Bashantek expenditure pattern bears any resemblance at all to these series.

Equally relevant and no more available is information on the marginal elasticity of income expenditure or the way a squatter would spend, say, an additional increment in earnings of Tk. 100. A study in 1973 (Khan and Alam, 1973, pp. 10-11) revealed that under such conditions, squatter families would spend 46.4% on savings, 32.2% on food, 7.2% on clothing, 5.9% on rent, 2.2% on recreation, 1.9% on transportation and 4.2% on other things. It is virtually impossible to guess whether these values would have changed over time or not, or whether they were even an accurate reflection of reality at the time they were collected.

The 1978 UNCDF study did, however, attempt to estimate the propensities to contribute to housing expenditure by various income classifications. Although these are no more than estimates, they are incorporated into the present analysis on an annual basis in order to provide at least a crude estimate of repayment ability. The report presents the data in the form of a range, and to obtain a unique figure for each income category, the mid-point of this range is used.

As would be expected, higher income families would be able to contribute more to the repayment charges than low

Table 13.   Total Community Repayments Required on Mirpur

Interest rates	0%		5%	
Time period in years	10	33	10	33
Target population: 2,300 households				
Full repayment of infrastructure only including lease charge	Tk.1,090,200 ($92,680)	Tk.331,200 ($22,080)	Tk.1,409,900 ($93,993)	Tk.680,800 ($45,387)
Full repayment of infrastructure and land	Tk.1,478,900 ($98,593)	Tk.448,500 ($29,900)	Tk.1,913,600 ($127,573)	Tk.924,600 ($61,640)
Target Population: 3,500 households				
Full repayment of infrastructure only including lease charge	Tk.1,092,000 ($72,800)	Tk.332,500 ($22,167)	Tk.1,410,500 ($94,033)	Tk.682,500 ($45,500)
Full repayment of infrastructure and land	Tk.1,477,000 ($98,467)	Tk.448,000 ($29,867)	Tk.1,914,500 ($127,633)	Tk.924,000 ($61,600)

income families. Assume for the moment that such a rent allocation structure were feasible to implement and that rents were based on ability to pay. In that unlikely case, the number of families in an income classification multiplied by the annual amount they were able to pay would yield the total annual payment of that category to the repayment charges. The sum over all income classifications would yield the actual amount that could be paid by the community.

These figures are drawn together in Table 14. Although the data are actually relevant for no more than the 201 families that were surveyed in Bashantek by the CUS, for the purposes of this analysis these samples have been expanded to the two target populations of 2,300 and 3,500 families used in earlier calculations. It is assumed that other residents who might be attracted to the scheme would have a similar income distribution and ability to pay for housing expenditures as those in the Bashantek sample. The calculations for a target population of 2,300 families is shown in the upper half of the Table while the calculations for 3,500 families are shown in the lower half.

We can compare the community repayment collections that result from the differential rent system as shown in

Resettlement Project under Varying Assumptions (1978 costs)

8%		12%	
10	33	10	33
Target population: 2,300 households			
Tk.1,621,500 ($108,100)	Tk.945,300 ($63,020)	Tk.1,925,100 ($128,340)	Tk.1,338,600 ($89,240)
Tk.2,203,400 ($146,893)	Tk.1,283,400 ($85,560)	Tk.2,617,400 ($174,493)	Tk.1,817,000 ($121,133)
Target Population: 3,500 households			
Tk.1,620,500 ($108,033)	Tk.948,500 ($63,233)	Tk.1,928,500 ($128,567)	Tk.1,340,500 ($89,367)
Tk.2,201,500 ($146,767)	Tk.1,284,500 ($85,633)	Tk.2,618,000 ($174,533)	Tk.1,816,500 ($121,100)

Table 14 with the community repayment requirements shown earlier in Table 13. For the target population of 2,300 households, the lowest repayment is for infrastructure alone with no interest charges over a 33-year leasehold period, where the requirement is Tk. 331,200 ($22,080). Even using the differential rent system, the community could provide no more than Tk. 147,573 ($9,838), or less than 45% of the amount required, under this set of assumptions. At least in the early years, there would be no hope whatsoever of returning to the Government the full cost of the project at even a nominal rate of interest.

For the settlement with a target population of 3,500 households, a similar situation results. Again, the least expensive solution from the community's point-of-view is at a zero rate of interest over a 33-year period for repaying only the infrastructure. The community cost of this solution is Tk. 332,500 ($22,167) while the most that could be paid under the assumptions of a differential rent system is Tk. 224,595 ($14,973) or 68% of the requirement.

In fact, if one takes the total amount of rent that could be paid under such systems (the two totals shown in Table 14), assuming that this amount increased in proportion to

Table 14. Repayment Collections on the Basis of Differential Rents by Income Classification

Annual income (Taka/year)	Number of families	Average propensity to pay for scheme (Taka/year)	Total payment by Income Group (Taka/year)
Target Population: 2,300 households			
Less than 1200	309	12	3,708
1201 – 2400	309	36	11,124
2401 – 3600	812	36	29,232
3601 – 4800	378	84	31,752
4801 – 6000	252	96	24,192
6001 – 7200	92	150	13,800
7201 – 9600	114	210	23,940
9601 – 1200	23	255	5,865
Over 12000	11	360	3,960
		Total	Tk. 147,573 ($9,838)
Target Population: 3,500 households			
Less than 1200	470	12	5,640
1201 – 2400	470	36	16,920
2401 – 3600	1,237	36	44,532
3601 – 4800	575	84	48,300
4801 – 6000	383	96	36,768
6001 – 7200	139	150	20,850
7201 – 9600	174	210	36,540
9601 – 12000	35	255	8,925
Over 12000	17	360	6,120
		Total	Tk. 224,595 ($14,973)

the approximate annual increase in GNP that was occurring in Bangladesh at the time[2], that is, 6.7%, and compounded this increase forward into time, some rough idea of when such payments might be feasible would result[3].

This set of calculations, presented in Table 15, yields very discouraging results. For example, even with an interest-free loan and a 10-year lease period, the inhabitants of the community would not be able to meet the entire annual obligation for infrastructure plus lease charges until the thirty-first year, long after the expiration of their leasehold period. Once interest rates are charged, the results become even more discouraging from the financial viewpoint even with the inclusion of the hypothesized differential rent system. On the basis of this, one can hardly conclude that the project is financially feasible. Feasibility would only have been achieved if the income generation program could have led to rises in incomes significantly above those levels assumed.

A more traditional way of collecting a rental or pur-chase charge from the inhabitants would have been on the basis of a flat rate where everyone in the community had the same obligation toward repayment. The required sums for such schemes are readily computed. At a nominal interest rate of 8% repaid over 33 years with the assumption that infrastructure alone would be repaid and that land would be subject to a leasehold arrangement at 1978 rates, the annual charge per household for the community of 2,300 families would be Tk. 411 ($27) while for the target of 3,500 families it would be Tk. 270 ($18) per year.

The results are not unexpected as the flat rate elim-inates the subsidy from the better off to the poorer elements of the community that is an inherent part of the differential rent system. As even the more wealthy households within the community are assumed to be able to pay no more than Tk. 360 ($24), the 2,300 family cost excludes the entire target population while for the larger settlement, over 98% are unable to make the necessary payments in the initial years of the contract.

Even with an interest-free loan with equal payments over 33 years and similar assumptions regarding land tenure, the annual charges of Tk. 144 ($9.60) and Tk. 94 ($6.27) for the communities of 2,300 and 3,500 households respect-

Table 15. First Time Period in which Community Repayment can meet Requirements*
(Expressed in years in the future)

Interest rates	0%		5%		8%		12%	
Time period in years:	10	33	10	33	10	33	10	33
Target Population: 2,300 households								
Full repayment of infrastructure only including lease charge	+31	+13	+35	+24	+37	+29	+40	+35
Full repayment of infrastructure and land	+36	+18	+40	+29	+42	+34	+45	+39
Target Population: 3,500 households								
Full repayment of infrastructure only including lease charge	+25	+7	+29	+18	+31	+23	+34	+28
Full repayment of infrastructure and land	+30	+11	+34	+22	+36	+27	+38	+33

* Assumes differential rent policy and a 6.7 per cent compounded annual increase in family income.

ively would exclude a significant proportion of the target group. In the former instance nearly 90% would be unable to make the initial required payments while in the latter instance, the exclusion figure drops to no less than 78%. Hence, even with the most liberal repayment demands, a large majority of the target population would be unable to participate.

THE FEASIBILITY OF A FLOOD-FREE SITE

In this section the problem of site selection and its effect upon financial feasibility is considered. Frequently, in projects such as that planned for Mirpur, sites are selected from parcels of land owned by the state which seem to have limited alternative uses. In such instances, the site may not necessarily be appropriate for the project planned at that location and project costs might be expected to fall as other sites are considered. Was Mirpur such a case? Since the largest proportion of the Government's costs were concerned with the necessary earthwork operations (embankment, levelling, drainage) that were necessitated by the fact that the land allocated to the Mirpur project was subject to monsoon flooding, would financial feasibility have been improved by selecting a site for the resettlement scheme on flood-free land?

An obvious trade-off exists between these two alternatives within the Bangladesh context. Higher elevation land implies lower development costs but at the same time the cost of the land itself is initially higher. Although data do not exist to fully delineate the exact relationship between price and elevation, more basic information on the differential between high and low land does exist.

A study of the Savar area (Ahmeduzzaman, 1979) provides some idea of the differentials that exist. Savar is located on the extreme urban fringe of Dhaka, about 18 miles to the northwest of the city. It is no more than 8 miles from the site of the Mirpur Resettlement Scheme. Consequently, it is reasonable to assume that the price differentials between high and low land and the actual value of such types of land will not be too dissimilar.

Within the Savar area, it was found that historically high land is $1\frac{1}{2}$ to $2\frac{1}{2}$ times more expensive than low land.

In areas with poorer access to main roads and to neighboring urban centers, the 1978 price of high land varied from Tk. 60,000 to Tk. 100,000 ($4,000 to $6,667) per acre while low land varied from Tk. 30,000 to Tk. 60,000 ($2,000 to $4,000) per acre. More central areas of the administrative region resulted in the expected higher prices with the 1978 price of high land varying from Tk. 120,000 to Tk. 150,000 ($8,000 to $10,000) per acre while low land was Tk. 80,000 to Tk. 90,000 ($5,333 to $6,000) per acre. Hence, the ratio of high to low land in the remote areas of Savar ranges from 1.67:1 to 2:1 while more accessible plots range from 1.5:1 to 1.67:1.

It is difficult to equate the site allocated to the Mirpur Resettlement Scheme precisely to the areas studied in Savar. Although a major criticism of the selection of the site at Mirpur concerned its remoteness to central Dhaka, it is still more accessible than a site in Savar would have been. At the same time, the site has good access to the central areas of Mirpur itself. For the moment, let us assume that the price ratio of high to low land in Mirpur is similar to that in the more accessible areas of Savar. Taking the most cautious approach, one might specify that high land is twice as expensive per acre as low land and that high land of sufficient quantity is available in the Mirpur area for the settlement. Alternatively, one might wish to value high land at no more than 1.67 times the price of low land. What changes would occur in the cost figures that we have previously computed? Would a shift occur in the financial feasibility for the project under these assumptions?

Now, let us define two alternative sets of costs for the project that was sited on the low land. Alternative 1 might be termed the conservative pricing approach. Here it will be assumed that the relevant ratio of high land to low is 2:1. In the 1978 UNCDF scheme for Mirpur, 18.9 acres of the 87.0 acre site was to be occupied by the embankment. The first saving that would result in this alternative scheme would be the reduction of the project area from 87.0 to 68.1 acres. Obviously, the price per acre would no longer be the value Tk. 45,000 ($3,000) as used in later calculations by the Housing and Settlements Directorate, but, due to the use of flood-free land, twice that, or Tk. 90,000 ($6,000) per acre. The total cost of the plot under this alternative would then be Tk. 6,129,000 ($408,600).

In Alternative 1, the cost of the embankment would disappear as on high land it would be unnecessary. Similarly, pumping operations would be unnecessary. It is assumed that some sort of site grading and levelling, as well as drainage, would be required and under this alternative we might assume that the cost on both high and low land were the same, although it should be noted that this assumption would certainly play against the decision to build on high land as it is likely that both sets of costs would be greatly reduced, a situation that will be allowed in Alternative 2.

Alternative 2 involves a liberal approach to pricing policy for the scheme. In this instance, the rate of high to low land will be assumed to be 1.67:1, that is, at the lower end of the scale as revealed in the Savar data. Consequently, the price per acre of land is assumed to be Tk. 75,150 ($5,010) and with a requirement of 68.1 acres, the total land cost under Alternative 2 is Tk. 5,117,715 ($341,181). As in the previous high land example, an embankment and pumping arrangements would have been unnecessary under these assumptions.

In this case, specific allowance is made for the smaller demand for levelling and drainage due to the higher elevation of the land which would give better natural drainage and would make levelling less necessary. The UNCDF report specifically estimated that cutting and filling of 2 feet over 50% of the site area, amounting to an approximate volume of earth equalling 3,789,720 cubic feet by mechanized means would cost Tk. 2,273,832 ($151,589). Without a specific site for computations, the current estimate cannot approach this degree of precision. A similar situation exists for the proposed storm-water drainage at the Mirpur site. In lieu of these difficulties, it is assumed that the combined cost of grading, levelling and draining would be half as much on a high land site as on the low land site.

All other costs would be the same as in the case of Alternative 1. In both of the alternative estimates, it is assumed that the costs to be covered previously by UNCDF would also be covered by them in such a revised scheme on high land.

The costs to the Government for each alternative would be as shown in Table 16. The Table reveals that both sets of the high land costs lead to a lower cost per family under either set of target populations. Even in Alternative 1, which might be regarded as a sort of upper bound on the cost of the project on high land (while Alternative 2 forms what is probably a lower bound), total costs are no more than 69% of their level on low ground. In this case it is apparent that the benefit to be gained by building at flood-free elevations more than offsets the additional cost of more expensive land by a significant amount.

Even this move to high ground with the subsequent reduction of cost does not guarantee financial feasibility, particularly if interest is charged on the capital sum. It does, however, bring the project much closer to the break-even point. If Alternative 1 was to be made available on an interest-free basis over a 33-year period, with payment demanded for the infrastructure and a lease-charge being made for the land, the annual cost for each family on an equal-rents basis would be Tk. 54 ($3.60) for a target population of 2,300 and Tk. 35 ($2.33) for a target population of 3,500. In the former instance, 38% of the Bashantek residents could afford the scheme on the basis of 1978 incomes and in the larger settlement of 3,500 households, fully 87% would be able to afford the annual payments.

Alternative 2 would give more or less the same results. Although the drop in annual rental payments between the two alternatives is relatively large, the absolute poverty of the lowest income group in Bashantek, which is incidentally the only one excluded in the scheme with a target population of 3,500 households, is still too great to reach the necessary rent-paying ability.

However, with respect to Alternative 2, even if an 8% interest charge was made on Government-provided infrastructure, again assuming a leasehold charge for the land, then for the settlement of either 2,300 or 3,500 households, 38% of Bashantek residents could afford the charges.

Form this analysis, it is apparent that had the Mirpur Resettlement Project been sited on high rather than low land, financial feasibility would have been enhanced, even if the overall requirements in terms of affordability were not met. The required land area would have been lower, the cost of the embankment eliminated and the land development

Table 16. Alternative Government Costs for the Mirpur Scheme on High and Low Land.

Item	High Land Alternative 1	High Land Alternative 2	Low Land Actual estimates
Embankment	-	-	Tk.5,490,000 ($366,000)
Site grading	Tk.2,273,832 ($151,589)	Tk.1,136,916 ($75,794)	Tk.2,273,832 ($151,589)
Pumps/pumping station	-	-	Tk.1,300,000 ($86,667)
Drainage	Tk.221,640 ($14,776)	Tk.110,820 ($7,388)	Tk.221,640 ($14,776)
Roads/footpaths	Tk.693,158 ($46,211)	Tk.693,158 ($46,211)	Tk.693,158 ($46,211)
Water supply	Tk.891,875 ($59,458)	Tk.891,875 ($59,458)	Tk.891,875 ($59,458)
Sub-total	Tk.4,080,505 ($272,034)	Tk.2,832,769 ($188,851)	Tk.10,870,505 ($724,700)
Land	Tk.6,129,000 ($408,600)	Tk.5,117,715 ($341,181)	Tk.3,915,000 ($261,000)
Total	Tk.10,209,505 ($680,634)	Tk.7,950,484 ($530,032)	Tk.14,785,505 ($985,700)
Per household cost for 2,300 households	Tk.4,439 ($296)	Tk.3,457 ($230)	Tk.6,428 ($429)
Per household cost for 3,500 households	Tk.2,917 ($194)	Tk.2,272 ($151)	Tk.4,224 ($282)

cost greatly reduced. The analysis reveals the importance of the initial site selection decision in meeting resource constraints and hence improving the probability of successful implementation.

CONCLUSION

In this chapter, economics has moved into the spotlight. After initially comparing costs for the various projects which had been proposed as resettlement schemes in the Mirpur area, it was noted that the cost of the UNCDF scheme was high compared to the incomes of the target group. In fact, this is the most important housing issue in Bangladesh, as the majority of the population can afford to make no more than minimal contributions to their housing.

As originally envisaged, the project did not meet the criterion of financial feasibility. Even the use of differential rents, which were unlikely to be a feasible alternative to the standard rents approach, failed to cover more than a portion of the costs involved in the project.

The analysis demonstrated that the financial feasibility of the project could have been improved by considering alternative sites to the one actually chosen. By selecting a flood-free site, various major costs associated with the flooding problem could have been eliminated, yet even with this step, the potential returns of the project failed to meet the planned costs.

Other alternative ways of reducing cost might have been considered in the analysis. Rather than designing a project around housing which was provided by the sponsors, a site and service scheme might have been considered. The actual savings from such an alternative would have been fairly small, since most housing costs in the scheme were to be provided from an outside source and since the expenditure to be recovered by the Government of Bangladesh did not include this amount. Given the very skewed income distribution of the former squatters, even a substantial savings from a radical redesign of the project in favor of the site and services alternative, would have been unlikely to increase significantly the proportion of the community who could pay the required rents.

One can only conclude from a financial viewpoint that the proposed project could not overcome the resource constraint. As a result, from the outset, successful implementation was unlikely unless significant subsidies had been granted to the project by the Government which could not afford them. It would seem that once the decision was made to remove the squatters from Dhaka and resettle them in such a community, from a financial point-of-view, implementation difficulties were inevitable.

7. The Implementation of the Mirpur Project

The planning of the Mirpur project had been completed and the implementation process was about to begin. As should be evident from previous chapters, certain storm clouds were almost certainly on the horizon. In this chapter, we see how the story of Mirpur turns out.

Two major implementational issues are extracted for analysis[1]. The first section deals with the problems of coordination that arose during the process, attempting to assess the effect of the organizational linkages that were specified for the implementation and to see how the system worked. Within the analysis of coordination, an issue which inevitably arises concerns the problems that existed with respect to reaching agreement between the Government of Bangladesh and the United Nations Capital Development Fund on the project document and the results of this lack of agreement.

In the second section, the planner's framework for implementation analysis is necessarily widened as we direct attention toward the actual construction of the embankment that was to protect the resettlement scheme. Although some will argue that this element lies beyond the area of concern of the planner, it will be observed that many of the funda-mental problems that arose within the construction process might well have resulted from taking this narrow view during the planning process. The key issues which arise in this section concern the capability of the Bangladesh construction industry, the responsiveness to monitoring reports and the general framework of carrying out a technologically-sophisti-

cated project in a country where the ability and will to do so
may be lacking.

THE PROBLEM OF COORDINATION

The planning of the Mirpur Resettlement Project formally ended with the publication of the UNCDF consultants'
report in January 1978, but unfortunately a number of loose
ends remained. Formalized plans had been presented of the
layout for the scheme showing utilities, roads, drains and
housing areas. However, the final plans for certain infrastructural components, such as the sewerage system and
electrical connections and most importantly, the administrative arrangements for implementation, were still incomplete.

It seems probable that such incomplete plans could have
been absorbed into the implementation process under normal
circumstances but the construction process at Mirpur was
anything but normal. Initially problems arose because
confusion existed as to precisely who was responsible for
what. The Mirpur project was divided into three stages:
site preparation, site development and site management and
operation. As a result of the size and complexity of this
particular scheme, however, a number of other independent
agencies became involved in the work and in none of the
proposals that emerged from various sources were the exact
responsibilities of each fully delineated. A summary of the
responsibilities of these various organizations, as extracted
from various coordination and monitoring reports, is given as
Table 17.

The complexity of the situation was compounded when it
was discovered that Housing and Settlements thought their
primary role was to provide money for land development and
that UNCDF would provide the rest. Dhaka Electricity
Supply had assumed that Housing and Settlements would be
responsible for the electrical work while the Water and
Sewerage Authority eventually proved unwilling to commit its
own funds to providing a water supply. Yet in one sense,
as we shall see, all of this gets us very far ahead of our
story and on to grounds that, in the end, proved to be
largely hypothetical.

Table 17.   Mirpur Resettlement Project: Organizations
            Involved.

Finance
        Government of Bangladesh: domestic costs
        United Nations Capital Development Fund through
            United Nations Development Programme: imported
            items, housing

Overall Coordination
        Ministry of Planning

Supervision
        Housing and Settlements Division of Ministry of Public
            Works and Urban Development: site preparation
            and site development
        Ministry of Public Works and Urban Development: site
            management and operation

Implementation
        Housing and Settlements Division of Ministry of Public
            Works and Urban Development: site development,
            including embankment, pumping installations, roads
            and drainage (construction and maintenance carried
            out by contractors)
        Dhaka Water and Sewerage Authority: deep tube wells
            (with UNCDF financial assistance)
        Dhaka Electricity Supply: electricity (with UNCDF
            financial assistance)
        Bangladesh Development Board of Water and Power
            Development Authority: advisers to HSD on
            embankment
        Public Health and Sanitation: advisers to HSD on
            drainage
        Roads and Highways Directorate of Ministry of Rail-
            ways, Roads, Highways, and Road Transport:
            Roads
        Bangladesh Army: Roads
        OXFAM: construction, employment survey
        CONCERN: construction
        Bangladesh Rural Advancement Committee: construction

Operation
        Bangladesh Voluntary Service: to run schools
        Center for Urban Studies, University of Dhaka:
            monitoring

One of the most serious constraints upon the implementation of the Mirpur scheme was the less than enthusiastic response that emerged from certain departments of the Government to the scheme proposed by the UNCDF consultants. As a result, the formal agreement on the project between UNCDF and the Government of Bangladesh was not signed in 1978, and for that matter, remained unsigned for the entire period of this analysis. A number of reasons have been suggested for this situation (Khan, 1979). The necessary working arrangements between the Planning Commission, which was responsible for the overall supervision of the project, but also ultimately responsible for negotiation with UNCDF, and the Housing and Settlements Directorate of the Ministry of Public Works, were never established and, as a result, the project had a divisive rather than cementing effect upon their relationship.

When attempts were made at a later date to establish a technical committee to supervise the implementation of the process, both organizations pressed claims to chair that body, the Planning Commission's based upon their senior role in the nation's planning organization and the Housing and Settlement Directorate's (HSD) on their central role in the implementation of the scheme. Furthermore, the priority given to squatter community schemes by ' the two organizations were given significantly different weightings. The Planning Commission, with its overall responsibility for development planning in the nation accorded the Mirpur scheme relatively minor importance while HSD viewed it as much more of a mainline operation. Individuals within these organizations, however, sometimes took quite different views with certain high-ranking personnel from the Planning Commission arguing strongly in favor of the project.

Yet despite the lack of formalized agreement between the Government of Bangladesh and the United Nations, work started on the project as if such an agreement did exist and the Government disbursed funds and carried out portions of its own project responsibilities on the assumption that the United Nations delay in ratifying the agreement was a temporary condition. This resulted in another of the many ironies that occurred during the planning and implementation of the project, that one of the poorest countries in the world spent a fairly significant amount of money on the assumption that a development agency would eventually provide the committed funds to finish the project. Given that Bangladesh is clearly in the category of one of the ten poorest member countries in the United Nations, and that United Nations development programs gave priority to this category, in January 1978, this might have been a justifiable assumption. As the months passed with still no agreement on the project document, it is apparent in retrospect that far greater caution should have been shown. Such, however, was not the case and the implementation program as suggested in the consultants' report began more or less on time in order to complete the work by the beginning of the 1978 monsoon.

During the first five months of the construction work, however, there is no evidence that any real effort was made either to coordinate the work that was to be carried out among the various organizations that were involved in implementation or to resolve the remaining organizational loose ends. In fact, it was not until June 1978 that a coordinating committee was established and even then the operating terms of reference and organizational structure of that committee were not resolved.

The committee itself was established as a result of a crisis. By May, although the embankment was not totally completed, it was at least physically in place. The UNCDF design consultant had returned to Bangladesh for a follow-up visit to the project. On an inspection visit to the site it was discovered that a serious slippage had occurred at a number of points along the embankment and that, in effect, the dike, built as it was on what had previously been rice paddy production land, was sinking[2].

With the realization that the entire project was on the verge of possible disaster and that the onset of the monsoon rains could only be a few weeks ahead, under the instigation of the UN personnel in Dhaka (despite the fact that the UN was not yet contractually involved in the project) a co-ordination group was established. Over the next seven months, a period which could be characterized as one of almost continual crisis on the project, a total of 25 meetings were held by the committee.

The primary participants were representatives from HSD, the United Nations (including personnel from both the permanent UN mission in Dhaka and the various relevant technical assistance projects) and spokesmen from the three most involved voluntary organizations - BRAC, OXFAM and

CONCERN. In the end, the chairmanship of the committee was easily resolved as no representative of the Planning Commission attended until the sixteenth meeting in December 1978, when the Planning Commission Member for Physical Infrastructure attended and he was invited to chair that particular meeting.

In the course of these sessions, a serious effort was made to resolve the remaining outstanding issues facing the project. At the same time, however, the minutes of these meetings revealed the problems that affected the effectiveness of the various organizations that were involved and the uncertainty that surrounded their own roles. For example, a community development project had been envisaged jointly involving OXFAM and BRAC to develop organizations and the public involvement of the Bashantek residents prior to the actual move to the Mirpur site. In the original plan it had been expected that OXFAM would provide financial support and play a supervisory role while BRAC would shoulder responsibilities for staff training, playing a sort of middleman's role between the project planners and local inhabitants. OXFAM discovered, however, that due to staff constraints, they were unable to participate in more than a financial support manner, leaving BRAC with added responsibilities. BRAC was already committed to operating labor-intensive land levelling projects on the interior of the embankment. As a result, that organization also considered itself to be short of supervisory staff, but as a result of OXFAM's generosity, not short of money. At the same time, however, they were reluctant to recruit further personnel for the project until they were certain that the Government was committed to the proposed moving date, and all of this, of course, was in turn dependent upon the UN joining the project[3]. Consequently, many of the organizational problems faced by the participating groups were circular in nature, dependent ultimately on parties that were in some cases not even participating in the committee sessions.

On certain issues such as the type of sanitation system to be incorporated in the project, the committee discussions were extensive[4]. Given the presence on the committee of engineers from OXFAM, CONCERN, HSD and the United Nations, these debates were highly sophisticated, dealing with issues in far more detail than other discussions, such as that of organization.

Although the original UNCDF Report recommended an aqua-privy for each house to be installed once the training program on their proper use and maintenance was completed, the sewerage disposal system to be associated with them had to be determined by the Committee. Six distinct systems were investigated by the group. Three of these were open systems with drainage into ponds within the proposed settlement while three others were closed systems requiring seepage pits and septic tanks.

Initially a decision was made to deal with the effluent by retaining it in a 24 cubic foot tank below each aqua-privy for partial decomposition by normal septic tank action before disposal of the partially-treated effluent into the storm water lake drainage system. The cost of this system was estimated to be Tk. 1,800,000 (US $120,000). Not all members of the Committee were satisfied with this decision, however.

The NGO responsible for the liaison between residents of Bashantek and the planners, BRAC, reported the reservations toward the scheme of the future residents, in one of the few instances where the target population appears to have been consulted on components of the project. They argued that when such effluent in sludge form is disposed of in a water course, it is still offensive and could pose a health hazard. Since the ponds were traditionally used by Bengalis for washing, fishing and even recreation, the future residents themselves were reported to be surprised that they might be deliberately polluted and were opposed to the idea. The BRAC statement went on to express doubt as to whether the system was better than what the people could do for themselves, arguing that "if dangerous effluent is to be discharged into the lakes it might be simpler and cheaper to install simple overhang latrines at the lakeside"[5].

On the basis of these arguments, an alternative closed system was selected, involving septic tanks and seepage pits. Of the six systems initially considered this was not only the most expensive, costing an estimated Tk. 2,223,100 ($148,207) in 1978 prices, but also the most technically sophisticated[6].

When coupled with the proposed inclusion of actual aqua-privies, it is increasingly apparent that the planners, engineers and designers who participated on the Committee viewed the Mirpur settlement as far more than a temporary solution to the Bangladesh squatter resettlement problem. In effect, they were designing what might well have been the most technologically-advanced new community in Bangladesh. At the same time, it appears that since the serious problems of financial feasibility and cost recovery must have been known at the time, the economics of the situation was given a lower priority in these deliberations than such technological aspects. Had their plans and ideas been successfully completed, there seems little doubt that the settlement might well have been a model community that would have been of interest to a wide range of Third World nations as a possible solution to their own urban problems. There was, however, a major impediment beyond economic feasibility that stood between the dreams and aspirations of the planners and the final state of the project. This impediment was the embankment, the first stage in the implementation process and the stumbling block that turned dreams into nightmares.

CONSTRUCTING THE EMBANKMENT

To many planners, once the drawings of layouts and infrastructural items are completed they consider that their job is largely completed. Although they may make periodic site visits to discuss progress with the construction team, and certainly they would plan to attend the "grand opening" of the scheme upon completion, once the builders move in, the traditional responsibilities of the planners rapidly fade away.

This view of the roles of the respective parties who are involved may work fairly well on large construction projects in countries with a highly competent building industry, where blueprints and plans can be correctly interpreted and acted upon and where the construction team can make allowances and compensations for minor oversights excluded from the plans for a scheme. In many development projects, however, far greater integration between the planning and the implementation process is required to assure that a successful outcome results from the endeavor.

In fact, the link between planning and implementation can in any given set of circumstances be critical. If the link is weak, the project can go badly astray. In the construction of the embankment which was designed to protect the Mirpur Settlement from the annual monsoons, there is some evidence that this link was less than fully developed and that this was at least in part responsible for some of the subsequent problems that resulted.

Planners frequently assume that the construction team carrying out the projects they have designed are capable of following their instructions and timetables. Is this always the case? In the Mirpur example, did not the state of the construction industry itself have something to do with the problems of implementing the scheme? And given this knowledge of that sector's inherent problems, should not early warning bells have rung in the planning offices, drawing attention to the need for close supervision and monitoring of the construction process?

Let us turn briefly to a review of the state of the Bangladesh construction sector to see if these necessary warning signs might not have already been present when work began on the Mirpur project in January 1978.

As the evolving development programs of Bangladesh shifted increasingly from the compilation of strategies and ideas to the actual placing of bricks and mortar, the efficiency and capability of this sector of the economy was viewed with increasing alarm. In February 1977, the World Bank's Resident Mission in Dhaka actually wrote to the Government suggesting the need for accelerated efforts to improve the efficiency of the construction sector which absorbed over 70% of all public investment funds and offering technical assistance as a means of upgrading the industry.

In this instance the Government responded positively to the suggestion and in November and December 1977, a time that coincided with the UNCDF mission, a World Bank advisory mission visited the country. Their report (World Bank, 1978) provides one of the most comprehensive sources of data that exists upon the Bangladesh construction sector and many of their findings are directly relevant to the study of the implementation process of the Mirpur Resettlement Scheme.

A number of inherent problems were identified which severely constrained the sector's capability of meeting the demands placed upon it by national plans that involved extensive public works projects. Most work on major projects financed by Government are executed by private contractors drawn from a pool of firms that numbers about 10,000 and is growing rapidly. These range from very small family operations to huge, well-managed firms capable of undertaking all but the very largest of projects. At the same time, however, there is a very serious shortage of experienced personnel, particularly at the middle level in the executing Government agencies and at the level of site managers and foremen in the constructions firms, which impedes the more expeditious use of the existing abundant labor supply.

The Bank's report suggests that to achieve project success the manager should have full control over the necessary inputs for the job, such as manpower, equipment and materials. Yet much of the equipment required for various jobs is held by Government agencies who in turn lease it out to contractors. Even then it may not be available when required and may not be properly maintained. This can involve extensive delays in actually making the equipment available on site. Since the operators of the equipment themselves are Government employees rather than employees of the construction firm, many tend to feel no compunction of helping the contractors in meeting the deadlines imposed upon them by the executing agency in the Government (World Bank, 1978, Annex 6, p. 2).

A similar situation exists with respect to the necessary materials required for such jobs, and in the case of Mirpur, where imported foreign materials were to be crucial at various strategic points in the implementation process, this factor is particularly relevant in the present analysis. Some contracts between Government and contractors specify that the necessary building materials are to be provided by the contracting agency and that payment to the contractor specifically excludes these charges. The contractor is consequently dependent upon Government for making certain that materials are available when required, which in the case of foreign-supplied inputs can require long and closely coordinated lead times.

Both of these factors have a significant effect upon the performance of the contractors in their work and even upon the decision as to whether to pursue labor- or capital-intensive construction methods. As the World Bank mission report observed (1978, Annex 4, p. 5), "since the con-

tractor is not entitled to any compensation of his costs
caused by failures of the employer to provide equipment and
materials as required by the contractor to perform
efficiently, he is at the mercy of the engineers-in-charge
and has little incentive to develop his competence for
improving field operations". The result can be a situation
such as that described by Huq of "the Municipality carrying
out bituminous carpeting on main thoroughfares of the city
with pots, pans and tools resembling the accessories of
ancient witchcraft"[7]. The situation also profoundly affects
the relations between Government agencies and the contractors, leading the World Bank to conclude (1978, p. 3)
that "workers distrust one another, contractors distrust the
Government officials, who in turn distrust everyone".

One can but conclude that very serious problems
existed within the construction sector. Although the World
Bank report was not published until after the construction
work at Mirpur had begun, these problems were of general
knowledge to almost everyone who was concerned with
supervising building projects well before its publication and
the planners should have made allowance for such constraints
in the initial schemes that were devised at the site. Unfortunately, such allowances were not made. As we have
already noted, five months of the implementation schedule
had passed before one of the UNCDF consultants made a
follow-up visit and discovered the slippages that had
occurred on the embankment.

Once discovered, specific instructions were given to
revise the design of the embankment at this slippage point
from the originally prescribed 1:2 gradient to one that was
1:6, involving an addition of layers of earth on the side of
the dike to provide a counter-balancing weight and a
cessation of adding earth to the top as it was merely rolling
over the side and into the rising monsoon flood waters and
away. Furthermore, sketches were prepared detailing how
bamboo pilings should be inserted in a parallel line 150 to
200 feet on either side of the weakened portion of the dike
to retard further slippage.

At this particular point in the construction process, a
new set of monitoring information becomes available for
assessing the implementation of this project. Prior to this
date, the embankment construction had proceeded with
minimal technical supervision other than that which could be

provided by HSD which, while efficient at constructing
housing, was inexperienced at building embankments. This
new data were a series of embankment construction monitoring reports[8].

These reports allow us to trace through the response
process to problems which arose with respect to this single
most essential element of the entire scheme. The reports
assist in isolating one of the most crucial faults in the
design of the implementation process, that being the lag in
response of the construction team to respond to problems
that arose during the building process. If a delay in
responding to such reports is found to exist, then it is
apparent that a serious flaw exists in the implementation
procedures. This flaw is particularly significant in a
situation where a vital element of the project, such as
construction of the dike, is crucially dependent upon rapid
response to such reports. For this reason, detailed attention to the content of these reports seems worthwhile.

Although 600 laborers and 50 boats were engaged in
earthwork and turfing various segments of the embankment,
the response to the most critical of the problems which had
arisen at that stage was slow in coming. A month passed
before the necessary remedial work began. Unfortunately,
the quality of the work undertaken did not meet the standards expected by the inspection team who reported that the
bamboo pins were being driven haphazardly in no particular
pattern by means of small ineffectual hammers. Earth was
still being dumped over the crest of the dike, increasing its
weight still further and, as a result, accelerating the
already existing rate of subsidence. Perhaps even more
serious, a second segment of the dike, 250 feet in length,
was discovered to have subsided by three feet. This
settlement was thought to have been due to "shrinkage",
although the report indicates that soil test boring reports
requested when the original break was discovered were still
unavailable.

By now, the monsoon rains were well underway and the
external flood levels were rising daily. By July, however,
the floods were still at a relatively low level consequently
giving the construction force time to make the essential
repairs. Still, the inspection reports indicated that progress
was slow. At the height of the crisis it was reported that
650 laborers brought to the site from Tangail, 30 miles to

the north of Dhaka, were preparing to depart for a five-day religious festival. Although the contractor assured the site inspection team that replacements would arrive for the period, doubts existed as to whether they would indeed join the workforce and, in fact, they were not replaced.

Although no further subsidence had occurred on the two already discovered areas of slippage, partly as a result of overdue remedial action, a third more serious break was discovered in a 185 foot segment of the dike that had dropped fully five feet. As a result of the drop, the crest height of the dike was no more than one foot above the outside flood level. Given that the River Turag was expected to rise from three to six inches per day throughout the month of July, it was apparent that the situation at this point was critical. To insure that the necessary steps were being taken to repair the damage, the inspectors reiterated the need to expedite the carrying out of soil bearing tests at 50 foot intervals along the weakened lengths of the dike.

By the end of that month, although the three pre- viously discovered slippages had been more or less arrested, the total number of breakages in the dike had risen to six. One of these was a 200 foot length of the embankment which had sunk by up to three feet. In this instance, and at a second point as well, the probable cause was that the work force had been dumping clay over slender sections of the dike with no regard at all for the prescribed slope of the side. In fact, the slopes were estimated to be less than 1:1 compared with the originally intended 1:2 slope.

Two months after the discovery of the breaks in the dike, the recommended short-term remedial measures appear to have been implemented and no further visible signs of deterioration took place. Nevertheless, the dike itself, even though the original intended construction period had been stretched from 12 to 26 weeks, was at no point less than 5 feet below the revised design height.

Once the monsoon flood levels resided, attention was turned from the short-term problems of trying to keep the flood waters out of the interior of the embankment to attempting to rescue the project. The time frame for completion had shifted significantly as well, for now we find reference to hopes that the project could be completed by the 1979 monsoon. The report on the visits to the site again mention the need for soil bearing tests at the points of breakages to determine the depth of the underlying peaty-clay soil that had resulted in the slippage.

This reference to the need for soil bearing tests raises an interesting point. Despite the fact that the embankment was being constructed on paddy land that was by definition little more than a soggy bog and that two weeks of January 1978 had been devoted to a "survey and detailed design" stage of preparation and even given the colossal weight of the proposed embankment itself, no weight bearing capacity test was made on the soils over which the embankment was to be located. Even given this obvious oversight, as already noted, instructions were given to carry out these essential tests as soon as the break had been discovered. Yet the story has now progressed to late October and we see a further detailed set of instructions being given on how they should be carried out. Wisely, the tests were ordered not only for the break points but also at 300 foot intervals along the entire length of the dike. Obviously, although the monitoring information was available, it was not being incorporated into the implementation process.

It was not until November that the test boring began. Even then, they got off to a very shaky start. Initially a portable drilling rig was brought to the site from the nearby Bangladesh Building Research Institute but was removed a week later before any holes had been bored due to the Eid religious holidays associated with the Moslem Ramadan. By 6 December, two drilling holes had been completed and work was underway on a third. Contrary to instructions which called for tests to be made to depths of two to three times the height of the embankment, roughly to a maximum depth of 80 feet, the soil testing team seemed to be trying to make up for previous errors by sinking their boreholes to a depth of 130 feet.

Although no construction activity was taking place at the time, there was evidence that local inhabitants were starting to view the embankment as a sort of local natural resource. The inspection team noted that the local people were stealing dirt from the dike to make guide banks for their own fish cultivation projects and called on HSD to increase their vigilance.

In the meantime, the test boring continued. A private firm was hired to supplement the team operating from the Building Research Institute in hopes of speeding up the drilling. Quick results were essential as the resectioning of the embankment at the six breakpoints, which literally involved totally removing the fractured sections and replacing them with fresh soil, was dependent upon the underlying bearing capacities. If those repairs could be planned by early December, it was thought that the actual restructuring, and subsequently the remaining construction on the project, could be completed before the onset of the 1979 monsoon.

Therefore, arrangements were made between the inspection team from the Bangladesh Water Development Board, who by this time had taken over virtually all planning and monitoring activities on the project, even if on an informal basis, and HSD, who remained as the executing agency for the Government, to have the results made available no later than 12 December. That date passed and the work was still not completed.

To expedite the remaining tasks, it was suggested by the representative of the Bangladesh Water Development Board that the boreholes at the remaining sites be made across rather than along the center line of the embankment. These instructions were made to the executing agency but were apparently ignored. In fact, this work was not completed until two months after the absolute deadline required to allow for future planning.

A second piece of information was required for the resectioning planning that proved equally elusive. In order to estimate the earth filling requirements and the ultimate height of the embankment, the planning engineers needed to know the exact elevation with respect to the sea level at the site. Although an elevation marker had been placed on the site it was discovered that due to the haste with which the survey preceding it had been carried out, the elevation had merely been transferred from another elevation estimate at a point three miles away without a back-check. These results were similarly delayed for a period of two months and, as a result, the time available before the monsoon for work on the necessary repairs was critically short. By mid-February 1979, the embankment had been under construction for a total of 54 rather than the 12 week period originally envisaged. In a sense, the project was no nearer completion than it had been a year earlier.

In the meantime, the Bangladesh economy had experienced another change of fortune which severely affected all public planning and building activity in the nation. In January 1979, the Bangladesh National Economic Council imposed a re-allocation of development resources from non-agricultural to agricultural pursuits. As a result of this, the annual allocation of the Housing and Settlements Directorate was cut by 40%.

The cutback in resources placed HSD in a serious dilemma. On the one hand it was inevitable that a cut of such magnitude would seriously impede a wide range of their on-going and proposed projects. On the other hand, although it might have been tempting for them to walk away from the Mirpur Resettlement Project in hopes of forgetting about the problem, a very large amount of money had been spent on the embankment and, for that matter, on the entire project. As the UNCDF had not signed the project document, everything that had been spent was Government of Bangladesh money and in particular HSD money.

Partly on the basis of this factor of sunk cost and partly because some personnel in the Directorate did indeed have a deeply-felt commitment to the project and because there was pressure from certain officials in the Planning Commission, they decided to go ahead with it, diverting their available budgetary allocation to it.

Consequently, at the beginning of March 1979, tenders were floated for the resectioning of the broken segments of the embankment and contracts were awarded. Given the urgency of the tasks, the contractors were given two months to finish their assignments and they were informed in writing that if they did not finish 50% of the specified work within the first month, their contracts would be cancelled.

Despite this apparently accelerated schedule, the first contractor did not arrive at the site until 7 April and by 9 April three had begun work. Even once all arrived on the scene, the inspection reports indicated that the quality of much of the work was being performed in an unsatisfactory manner or, to quote directly from the reports, they were working "half-heartedly". In effect, previous mistakes were being incorporated into the process. Superficial compacting was taking place and truckloads of unbroken clods were being dumped haphazardly on the top of the dike. By the end of the first month, the work was far behind schedule, but it appeared that the enforcement of previous threats by the executing agency was not being carried out.

The words "appeared that" are deliberately chosen in the previous sentence. The inspection report of 3 May 1979 was the last in the series due to a disagreement that had arisen between the embankment experts from the Bangladesh Water Development Board and HSD. After nearly a year of voluntarily providing advice and suggestions as to the correct way of continuing with the job, the inspection team withdrew from the exercise claiming that a continued association with the project would be of little use to the UNDP. Their feeling was that whatever advice they gave was ignored and their involvement on an unofficial basis was little more than a waste of time.

As it turned out, the work was more or less finished in the end. It was of more or less indifferent quality, a dike that crumbled further during the 1979 monsoons but that did not matter greatly because, since the project document had never been agreed, nothing was ever built inside it. By August, the project was considered to be a dead issue by the UNCDF, although occasional efforts were made over the next two years to try to revive it. The problem facing the Government of Bangladesh was what to do with an embankment that did not keep out the water.

Throughout the autumn of 1979 and into 1980, half-hearted pumping operations were maintained to clear the accumulated water from one side of a leaky dike to another, yet presumably no one had thought to tell the pumpers that they were no longer needed. In one sense, this final omission seemed symbolic of the entire exercise.

By 1980, however, it was plainly apparent that the high hopes of planners and engineers, both from Bangladesh and abroad, as well as the 2,000 or so squatter families designated to occupy the Mirpur site, would not be met. Scarce resources had been spent. Nothing had been produced. Could the problems which prevented the completion of the Mirpur project have been foreseen? How many could have been overcome if they had been anticipated?

IDENTIFYING WHAT WENT WRONG

An inherent difficulty in analyzing any project as complex as the Mirpur Resettlement Project is that when failure occurs it is usually impossible to attribute it to any single cause. Constraints upon implementation tend to be interrelated in that any given problem affects other areas adversely. In the final analysis, it is seldom one constraint that defeats the implementers, but the combined effect of many.

In the case of Mirpur, a specific site was selected for the location of the project. As a result of the site-selection decision, an embankment was required to protect it from monsoon flooding and this in turn involved relatively complex technology and a construction industry which had difficulty in meeting the standards set for it. Given climatic constraints, such as the regularity of the monsoon, only a short period of time was available for the completion of the project at that particular site. Again, because of the peculiar nature of the site, the solution was more expensive than might have been the case at an alternative location and this in turn undoubtedly adversely affected the enthusiasm of certain parties to the decision. Finally, because the site required complex solutions, the coordinating requirements of the implementation process were far more complex than would otherwise have been the case, and hence scheduling became an important issue.

Perhaps the most straight-forward manner to summarize the difficulties that were encountered is to examine somewhat more closely this problem of scheduling and to see how it was affected by the conditions of the site.

One of the most important reasons for the lack of agreement between the UN and the government bodies concerned the problems that occurred during the construction of the embankment. Back in January 1978, the UNCDF consultants had confidently felt that the implementation of the project could be completed by June 1978, prior to the onset of that year's monsoon. The crucial item in the construction process was the 6,100 foot embankment that had to be completed before other infrastructure could be put in place. The importance of the dike was partly due to the fact that soil from the interior of the site would be required for it and partly because once the monsoon rains began in

May and June, without it, everything was likely to be flooded. It was expected that the embankment could be completed within five months, that is, by 1 June 1978. This allowed one month for its detailed design, three months for constructions and one month at the end for turfing to prevent erosion.

The provision of infrastructure was expected to begin by 15 February. Once the interior of the site was levelled and the tubewells sunk, work on the drainage, water, sanitation, electrical and road circulation system could be started. Each component of these systems was staged over a three and one-half month schedule, with a deadline for completion set on 1 June 1978.

Concurrently, the community building and shelters were to be constructed in the period between 1 April and 31 May. The OXFAM/BRAC employment survey and the organization necessary for the move from Bashantek to Mirpur was scheduled for completion by the end of June.

A parallel schedule was devised showing the time at which funds had to be made available by the UNCDF in order to allow imported materials to be obtained to meet the proposed implementation schedule. Thus the components of the water supply required $86,667 to be available for orders to be placed in February; the $36,936 for the materials for the construction of the drain covers had to be available by March, and so on through the various ingredients that were required for roads, footpaths, water points, sanitation, street lighting, housing, community facilities and the other contributions by UNCDF.

The construction schedule that was proposed seems, in retrospect at least, to have two major potential problems. The first of these was its tightness in terms of time available for each step. All necessary monies had to be made available by precise dates and rigid deadlines existed at each stage if the project was actually to be completed in time for occupation by the beginning of the monsoon period. Although a single delay in the provision of one of the less essential items, such as concrete for the drain covers, would not irrevocably delay the schedule, other components were potentially far more critical.

Directly related was the second characteristic of the implementation schedule which was that the physical components of later items in the schedule were entirely dependent upon a linkage of construction deadline dates of other items on the agenda. Hence, the water reticulation system could not be started until the water points were constructed and these in turn were dependent upon the successful completion of the deep tubewells. Most crucial of all, in that every other item in the scheme depended upon its successful completion, was the embankment. Obviously at an alternative flood-free site, these constraints would have been very much less severe.

It was envisaged that this set of interrelated activities, expressed in terms of systems analysis, would subsequently flow into one another with the ultimate output being a living community. Such scheduling is anything but unusual and indeed systems analysis itself is a powerful planning tool. Yet before such a scheme can be applied on a development project, one must clearly understand the inherent assumptions that it involves. Such analysis assumes that the specified tasks can be accomplished in the time allowed for them. If a deadline is overrun, then the entire schedule must be revised. In order to meet the deadlines, it would appear essential that all participants must be genuinely pledged to the schedule. Furthermore, all materials, equipment and manpower required to carry out the construction must be available on the site at the time required or else time must be explicitly included in the schedule for their requisition.

Unfortunately, in the original UNCDF report explicit account of these underlying assumptions seems to have been ignored. No room was allowed in the schedule for the flexibility that would have been required to account for delay in the construction of the embankment, or for that matter, for any other piece of essential infrastructure. Similarly, although timetables were provided to suggest dates when funds would be available for the ordering of essential inputs into the project, no estimates were made of the lead time required to assure that vital supplies were available on site when required, nor allowances suggested to account for possible delays in delivery. The terms of reference for the consultants specified that (UNCDF, 1978, p. 1) the design consultant was "required to cooperate with Government and other agencies involved in establishing suitable design standards for the project and to prepare the necessary drawings, specifications and estimates for the physical planning of the resettlement project" and that the financial analyst was "to review the direct construction costs and budget with the design consultant, to examine leasehold arrangements with the Government and to assess the relationship of the squatters' income to the standard of amenities". In terms of their official assignments then, the two consultants actually went beyond their terms of reference in making the detailed suggestions that they did put forth.

It seems that we have here an inherent weakness in planning thought concerning not only the process of implementation itself but more importantly with the establishment of a satisfactory framework within which implementation can take place. One often hears, particularly in the Third World and not always facetiously, that "planners plan and engineers implement". The missing link is the connection between the two. Who sets the framework for the final stage and with what degree of detail? In the case of the Mirpur scheme, it is apparent that this vital element was missing entirely. Already we have seen evidence of this omission at one level: the failure to take soil bearing tests before beginning the earthwork for the construction of the embankment. A second element of this omission obviously concerns allowance for the necessary lead times required to provide materials where needed at the proper time. Yet even these two areas of omission are far more complex than they appear, for each involves a whole series of interrelated decisions, any one of which, if arriving at an incorrect conclusion, can seriously delay the overall implementation schedule of the project.

At a belated stage, personnel involved with the Mirpur Project realized this and attempted to take various steps to remedy the earlier omission. At a meeting of the Coordination Committee on 21 November 1978 it was concluded that without a complete sequential list of tasks required for the project and the estimated time for each one, successful completion of the project was impossible.

The results of this analysis, presented to the Committee a month later, were based on the assumptions that the embankment would eventually be successfully completed, that the UNCDF would indeed sign the project document with the

Government of Bangladesh and that the remaining implementation of infrastructural and shelter elements would be carried out. It did not account for the unforeseen financial cut-backs which would be announced three weeks later.

The result was a far more realistic and detailed listing of the tasks and decisions which remained. With respect to the embankment alone, 242 separate tasks were identified by the Coordinating Committee. These were of varying size and any one of them could conceivably have acted as a stumbling point in the implementation process, imposing delays, technical complications and organizational disputes among the participants.

Viewed in this manner, what had previously been considered to be a relatively straightforward scheme of providing an embankment, community facilities and infrastructure, had become an extremely complex project indeed. The reason why it had been proven impossible to fit all of these implementation tasks together in a six month period between January and June 1978 was, perhaps for the first time, understood. Perhaps it was indeed something more than merely forgetting to carry out soil bearing tests.

CONCLUSION

It is likely that even in technologically-advanced societies the building of a new town in such a short period with such previously unrecognized interrelated constraints would have proved impossible. There was the experimental nature of the concept in a Bangladesh environment, the lack of experience with such projects by the executing agency, a difficult site that itself contained economic and technological implications, the problems experienced by the contractors working on site in not really understanding what was going wrong all around them, and the lack of project coordination at the critical early stages of the implementation process. It is hardly surprising therefore that the original timetable could not be followed. It is because of these reasons that the Mirpur Resettlement Project came to such an unhappy ending. Given the analysis here, and admittedly hindsight is always more illuminating than foresight, it would seem that most of these factors should have been foreseen and allowance made either to overcome them directly or to circumvent them.

Perhaps comparisons can be made to the other two resettlement projects at Tongi and Demra. Of course there were complications at these locations as well. The site at Tongi was far from ideal when the project began. Considerable filling was required before it could be inhabited, yet the technology involved was far simpler than that required to make the Mirpur site usable. Demra was even more straightforward. Neither required the complicated kind of flood-protection that was planned for Mirpur. At the end of the day, the projects at Demra and Tongi succeeded while the one at Mirpur never got off the ground.

The community development plans and the coordination requirements for Demra and Tongi were never thought of as being as complex as those proposed for Mirpur. The level of services planned was very much lower and, as a result, they were cheaper to build. At these two locations, however, the communities were not only completed but they have thrived. It is hard to avoid the conclusion that the simplicity of the plans had something to do with this as it reduced the likelihood of encountering constraints upon implementation which would prevent the successful completion of the project.

8. The Way Ahead: Planning for Implementation

The Mirpur experience is representative of circumstances that arise on development projects in all parts of the Third World. Projects which could lead to real improvements in the lives of people are designed, yet in the implementation process, frequently fall short of the high objectives set by government officials, planners and engineers. The in-depth analysis of the Mirpur project has been presented in order to lay bare the various kinds of constraints which retard implementation. Once identified, it was hoped that such impediments could be classified and solutions for overcoming them found so that waste of scarce development resources could be avoided at other projects in the future. Because impediments to successful project implementation occur not just in Bangladesh, but throughout the Third World, it was hoped that prescriptions for improvement might have fairly general applicability. Throughout this analysis, the assumption has been made that if constraints to implementation could be anticipated, the planning process could be designed to take account of them, thereby avoiding many of the kinds of problems which disrupted the Mirpur project.

In the opening chapter five sets of forces were identified which might have been expected to constitute constraints upon the implementation process. These were the effect of poor organization, resource shortages, lack of cultural understanding, inappropriate technology and inadequate public participation. Let us return to these five problem areas and see just what each contributed to the failure of the Mirpur project. At the same time, however, consideration should be given to the broader question of determining what could have been done to circumvent these particular effects.

ORGANIZATIONAL ISSUES

Organizational issues affect the implementation process in a number of distinct ways. Possibly the most critical time period in the implementation procedure, and the period where organizational structures are likely to be least developed, is at the very outset of the process.

Mirpur clearly confirms this suggestion. The most crucial time period for things to go wrong was between the start-up of construction and the discovery of the first slippage in the embankment. At that early stage, not all parties were even yet involved in the construction, yet from the time that the break in the dike was discovered, the fate of the project was effectively sealed. It would have been very difficult indeed to have salvaged it after that point simply because it would virtually have required going back to the very beginning and starting again.

At this embryonic stage of the implementation process, all participants were dependent upon the organizational planning elements included in the Mirpur resettlement scheme plan. As noted in Chapter 7, there were a number of loose-ends at the end of the planning process with respect to coordination, allocation of responsibilities and financial liability, and their combined effect resulted in the less than optimal implementation framework.

The second point where organizational factors played against successful completion of the project was in the response to the monitoring reports on the construction of the embankment. Once the crisis had emerged and a monitoring framework established, there was no authority with the power to enforce adherence to these reports. Literally months passed between the time a remedial step was suggested and a response was made by those responsible for construction. The fault in this instance undoubtedly lies with the on-site coordination authorities of the project. Although those responsible for the planning were involved in attempts to rectify the situation, due to the short term nature of their contractual obligations to UNCDF, these efforts proved ineffective.

A Coordination Committee was formed at the first sign of crisis, yet one cannot help but wonder why it had not been formed earlier. A review of the minutes of that group suggested that they viewed their responsibilities primarily in terms of planning various outstanding elements of the project rather than insuring that the executing engineers on site enforced adherence to the suggestions in the monitoring reports.

In studies that have been made of the planning process, very little thought has been directed toward thinking about what to do when those monitored do not respond to the process. Has such an event never happened before? In the case of Mirpur, enough was known about the state of the construction industry to move such events out of the category of randomness and into a new area where a high probability of difficulty seemed to exist. In effect, what was needed was far closer supervision, tightening even more closely the links between planning and implementation. Yet perhaps this was impossible where the planning was primarily carried out by international, short-term consultants, while the construction was the responsibility of local firms.

On the broader scale, it would appear that what was lacking in the Mirpur project was an adequate framework within the original plan for implementation of the project. This deficiency has relevance in terms of planning methodology: theoretically-inclined planners have devoted considerable effort to self-contemplation, undertaking detailed attempts to analyze what planners do and how they go about it. Most of this effort has been devoted to the planning process itself with only relatively recent attention being directed toward the implementation processes. Even rarer have been attempts to identify the linkages between these two fundamental activities and yet it was precisely within this area that important sets of problems occurred on the Mirpur project. Project implementers were expected to rectify the situation that had been left by the project planners and fill in the void that existed between the two areas. In other instances, it appears that the problems were merely assumed away.

Much of the difficulty that was encountered at Mirpur was due to the lack of a framework to insure coordination among participants. Although a fairly large number of organizations, government departments and contractors were expected to contribute to the project on a rigid time schedule, the mechanism to guarantee that this happened was not established until it was too late. As a result, the project was probably doomed before construction began.

With respect to organization, it is apparent that impediments arising within this area are readily traced to deficiencies in the planning process. A successful plan is one which ties up these organizational loose-ends and specifies the role of each body involved in implementation. It identifies financial responsibilities and insures that each contributor has agreed to its role within this sphere before implementation begins. If coordinating committees are to be required, the plan includes provision for them. In addition, rather than merely specifying that a monitoring of progress should be carried out, the plan identifies the monitoring authority and also sets forth the chain of command which will insure that a response is made to such monitoring.

In cases where short-term consultants contribute to vital elements of the planning process, the plan should clearly identify local counterparts who have the power to make necessary amendments to the plan if this should prove necessary during the implementation process to insure the built-in flexibility that is a prerequisite of successful project planning. Had these points been included in the Mirpur plan, many of the impediments that adversely affected implementation in this instance could have been successfully side-stepped.

RESOURCES

The Mirpur project demonstrates the financial vulnerability of any development project in a country as impoverished as Bangladesh. In poor nations, even small projects are expensive in terms of scarce resources. Here, however, international experience would seem to be able to make a contribution. If costs are indeed treated as a variable and if financial feasibility is as unlikely as we have seen, it would appear that the obvious answer is to reduce expenditure until the two economic forces are somewhat closer to equilibrium.

This is, however, not to suggest that full cost recovery should necessarily have been achieved in this particular project. The mere fact that UNCDF was willing to donate US $610,098 is evidence of a subsidy and a legitimate one under the circumstances. In a country such as Bangladesh, the poor simply cannot afford to make substantial, or even unsubstantial contributions to their housing. If a government decides to disrupt existing housing patterns, i.e., resorts to squatter clearance, then an obligation would seem to rest upon that government to contribute something toward the new shelter expenses incurred. Although it is readily acknowledged that there is a legalistic argument involved here and that removal of those illegally occupying land may be a part of such an operation, it should not be forgotten that there is also a human argument to be considered. In the case of poor nations, squatting is rarely undertaken by deliberate design but rather out of desperation. This in itself would appear to be sufficient justification for a subsidy. Even a modest subsidy would go a long way.

Yet by considering project cost as a variable to be minimized, it would seem that even less expensive alternatives to resettlement might be discovered. At Mirpur, one such alternative might have been a consideration of upgrading. Had migrants to Dhaka in the period between 1971 and 1974 been directed to Government land which was not demanded for other uses, rather than merely being allowed to settle at any place they wished (recall that this is exactly what happened in Chittagong, where land was reserved for such purposes), the foundation of this cheaper solution might have been established. The existing housing could have been preserved and eventually services and infrastructure extended to these areas with the possibility even of some form of secure tenure.

Obviously not all countries face the same financial constraints. Perhaps the more wealthy among Third World nations, such as Malaysia, can afford to follow their policy of building to a minimum acceptable social standard. Perhaps in Zambia the recovery of all costs from sites and services project expenditure is within the realm of the possible. Yet in the poorer nations, subsidies, whether they originate in the form of grants from the international community, or from cross-subsidization from the rich to the poor, may be essential for the foreseeable future if real improvements in the living standards of the poor are to result at all. This

financial flexibility must be a built-in feature of the design
of Third World urban projects.

From the evidence considered here with respect to
Mirpur, it became increasingly apparent that financial
considerations played a secondary role to plan design and,
as a result, a project was devised which did not meet the
critical standards associated with financial feasibility. Had
the plan reflected the existing constrained economic situation
within the country, the form of the project might have been
quite different. Many of the more luxurious elements of that
plan would have been deferred to the future when incomes
might have been expected to rise. For example, despite the
obvious desirability of drain covers, and possibly even
provided housing, the money to be spent on these items
might have been better invested in the form of a direct
subsidy to the construction being financed by the
Bangladesh Government.

This would have required a new element of flexibility
from international funding bodies. Such bodies may be
correct to insist on progressive improvements in projects in
which they become involved. At the same time, however,
funding bodies must realize that the insistence on progressive improvement, which is expensive, may push local government authorities beyond their financial means. If this is the
case, as indeed it was in Mirpur, the outcome is likely to be
an abandoned project rather than one which meets the
objectives of the international organization.

CULTURAL UNDERSTANDING

Intercultural communication and appreciation, even
between various groups within a single country, is one of
the more difficult of planning and implementation problems to
overcome. If it cannot be surmounted, however, it forms an
extremely serious constraint to project success.

In the case of Mirpur, evidence of cultural misunderstanding was available long before the planners even arrived
to begin work on the resettlement scheme. The mere fact
that one group of people in the country, having control over
the power of the State, decided to remove another group of
people from the original squatter communities since they did
not hold such power, is adequate evidence to make the

point. From the review of middle- and upper-class attitudes toward the squatters discussed in Chapter 3, it is apparent that an understanding of the plight of the squatters simply did not exist. Had it existed, it seems unlikely that resettlement programs of this sort would have been contemplated in the first place.

The choice of a location for the resettlement schemes again is evidence of cultural misunderstanding. Peripheral sites, a considerable distance from inner city employment opportunity characterized not only the site at Mirpur, but Demra and Tongi as well. Surveys of squatter characteristics, not only in Bangladesh, but also at the international level, invariably agree that the kinds of jobs low-income squatters are most likely to hold are to be found not on the edges of cities but toward the middle. Yet when decision-makers in the Government of Bangladesh made the decision for resettlement locations, all five candidate sites, including the three that were actually used, were on the periphery of the city.

Once the planning process began, further evidence of cultural distance between the planners and those for which the plan was designed is available. Although the priority of the squatters was to improve employability and to minimize housing and commuting expense, the plan prepared for Mirpur thrust them firmly into the formal housing market and, had it been completed, imposed upon them the cost of such housing. Certainly the contrast in housing cost between the scheme at Mirpur and the squatter community in inner Dhaka, or even for that matter, at Bashantek, was significant. Although an employment survey was an integral part of the plan, serious doubts must exist as to whether the implementation of an employment program would have been any more successful than the implementation of the housing program. In the end, the employment program sank without a trace, much as the embankment had done.

An inherent problem exists in borrowing the plans and ideas that may be appropriate for one culture, and adjusting them for another culture, where they may not be appropriate at all. Expatriate consultants have to be particularly careful to avoid this trap. Building houses for the poor has been an effective way of solving housing problems in countries like the United Kingdom but that does not necessarily assure that it will work in poorer developing countries. Full cost recovery may be feasible in the upper income range of Third World nations, but there is little evidence to suggest that it will work at the extreme lower end of the income scale.

Within the Mirpur project, survey data were available which gave a fairly clear picture of the priorities of the target population. Although the plan itself gave some consideration to the points revealed, most of the plan-making effort was devoted to designing physical structures that went far beyond what might have been termed the cultural norm of Bengali squatter society.

Yet this was a minor problem in the overall scheme of things, especially when compared to what had happened before the planners began their work. Once the squatters had been removed from Dhaka by the Government, something had to be done to make their continued existence at a new location possible. Hence the real cultural gap occurred not so much in the plan itself but within the terms of reference given to the planners and the concept of such a new community itself. If, as the survey revealed, maximizing access to employment opportunity was the squatters' most important objective, building houses seems a very unusual way of meeting it. If a project is to be successfully completed, it must be appropriate to the target population. It must receive the enthusiastic support of government decision-makers as well as their cultural understanding. If all involved parties can agree on the concepts to be included in such a scheme, it is far more likely to be successfully implemented than would otherwise be the case.

APPROPRIATE TECHNOLOGY

The Mirpur study reveals that technology sometimes rears its head in strange ways. One might not initially have thought of the Mirpur embankment as a technological element. This is surprising, however, since even in an advanced country like the Netherlands, such embankments are considered to be technological accomplishments.

Technology slips into Third World projects by a number of routes. Expatriate consultants can be expected to make suggestions which are based upon their own past experiences, and these are frequently gained in technically-advanced environments. Local planners and engineers, particularly if trained abroad, may seek solutions with a high technical content rather than an indigenous one. After all, one frequently hears criticism of the phrase "intermediate technology" as representative of something which is no more than "second best".

The incorporation of technology into development projects is a complex issue. The first problem is to identify what constitutes technology and this in itself varies according to circumstance. Within the Bangladesh context, for example, embankments have been successfully incorporated into a number of flood control projects in various parts of the country. Hence there was no reason to believe at the planning stage of the Mirpur project that they could not be used to protect the proposed settlement. The crucial issue then, would appear to be whether the planning framework could be established to insure the successful completion of such a structure.

This planning framework was dependent upon the technical surveys required prior to construction of the embankment and the capability of those charged with building it. The detailed provision for the necessary surveys appears no where in the Mirpur plan. Yet this was an essential ingredient of the planning process. What might seem to be a good and innovative idea could prove to be the opposite if the planners themselves do not understand the prerequisite requirements for undertaking such a venture. In Mirpur, this seems to have been the case.

Even if the technical surveys had been carried out to the required degree of thoroughness, the second problem concerning capability of the builders remains. It is essential that designers have some influence upon the selection of contractors if innovative ideas are to be successfully incorporated into their plans. Designers, engineers and planners would wish to know whether the contractors had been involved in such projects in the past and how they had coped with complex specifications and about their responsiveness to the inevitable design changes which accompany such projects. There is no evidence to suggest that the project planners were so involved, or that they were even consulted.

Much of this difficulty again seems to boil down to a less than complete plan, one which assumed far more than was justified. It was the detail of the plan which was paramount in importance and it was this which was missing. Although it was the embankment where the major implementation difficulties arose, the potential pitfalls of other technological elements of the plan (aqua-privies, sewerage disposal system, water supply, drainage and pumping) might have proved equally detrimental had the embankment been completed. In this case, we will never know because the project was abandoned before other construction stages were reached.

The crucial issue is the identification of the planning elements which should be classified as technological. Once these are isolated, special care is required to insure that the plan adequately spells out how progress should be made with respect to them. If this cannot be done, such components should be avoided. At Mirpur, a far better solution would obviously have been to have selected a flood-free site where the entire problem of the embankment could have been avoided. As it turned out, it would have been a better idea to fill the site to above flood-level, even if this was the more costly solution to that problem.

PUBLIC PARTICIPATION

Had the squatters been consulted by Government authorities prior to their removal from Dhaka in 1975, it is unlikely that the resettlement scheme at Mirpur would ever have been contemplated. Consultation with the public can occur at a number of different stages and at each of these, its content varies significantly. In 1974, squatters might have been consulted to determine whether alternative locations for their settlements could be found which would have been acceptable both to the residents and to the Government. Even after they were transplanted to Bashantek, efforts could have been made to agree upon the type of living arrangements which would be best to integrate them into urban society. There is no evidence that any of these steps were taken.

Within the planning process itself, at certain critical stages, the former squatters might have been consulted to determine the desired form of their future community at Mirpur. Although a survey was made of the residents of Bashantek which at least revealed their own priorities, it would have been difficult to proceed strictly by this means. Surveys of this type are prepared by planners, or in the case of the Bashantek residents, by university personnel in cooperation with the planners. The questions posed may not be the appropriate ones and, as a result, the true feelings of residents may remain undetected.

The only real way to obtain the necessary information might be through public meetings where all points-of-view could be aired, hopefully in an unconstrained way. Even consultation with community leaders is dangerous as one never knows whether the so-called leaders are self-appointed or are expressing views which are untypical of those of the rest of the community.

There is very little evidence to suggest that any real effort was made to incorporate the public into the Mirpur planning process. At a belated stage, the Coordination Committee, through the Bangladesh Rural Advancement Committee, responded to the wishes of the Bashantek community with respect to the sewerage disposal system planned for Mirpur. By this time, however, it was too late to make any difference.

One cannot help but wonder whether the project would have had a different fate if full and open consultation with the residents of Bashantek had occurred throughout the planning process? Would the design priorities of the planners have been altered? What would have been the residents' reactions to the financial implications of the project? What proposals might they have made to reduce the costs to levels which they would be able to afford?

A key element of the plans for urban change in Third World cities would of necessity seem to involve the target population. Until genuine participation by the public in the decision-making on projects which significantly affect their own futures can be achieved, progress in such areas will remain elusive.

CONCLUSION

In this study, five impediments to successful urban project implementation have been identified. Through the use of a case study based upon Bangladesh experience, the

way in which these constraints - organization, resources,
cultural understanding, technology and public participation-
affect project planning have been explored. It has been
argued that in almost all planning situations, these factors
should be identifiable in advance. Therefore, the fundamental premise of the analysis has been that the problems
which result from these impediments could be avoided if they
were explicitly taken into account in the planning process.

Although these constraints and their effects have been
examined in terms of a single urban resettlement project,
there would seem to be ample justification for broadening our
conclusions to include projects across almost all sectors
associated with urban planning and across a wide geographical area as well. They are not unique to the planning
of the Mirpur resettlement project nor to Bangladesh, but
are universal. Within different environmental situations they
may take a somewhat different form, nevertheless they are
present to varying degrees in diverse types of projects. It
is for this reason that the detailed analysis presented here
is considered to be worthwhile.

Throughout the Third World serious problems have been
caused in recent years by rapid urbanization. Governments
and international organizations have set as one of their goals
the creation of projects to overcome the adverse effects of
this rapid growth of cities. Transport systems are being
built. Houses are being constructed or serviced sites are
being made available for residents to construct their own
houses. Markets are being designed. Center city redevelopment is taking place. Increases in employment opportunity
are being planned. In all of these activities the constraints
which affected the Mirpur project are present. Yet if
progress is to be made, they must be overcome. In no
country are resources plentiful enough to allow wastage to
occur. Third World projects which are designed to overcome
specific problems but which are failures in the implementational sense merely squander the limited resources and
opportunities which exist.

Although urban projects designed to assist the poor
may have special difficulties attached to them, particularly in
terms of finance, in one sense they are no different from
any other type of project. An adequate planning framework
is required, one which takes into account the foreseeable
difficulties which can otherwise plague the implementation

process.   Hopefully, discovering ways of conquering these constraints should lead to greater success in alleviating the urban problems facing developing countries.

Footnotes and References

CHAPTER 1

Footnotes

1. Although Waterston's book is still considered the classic
   in the development field, similar views have been
   expressed more recently by Killick (1976, pp. 161-166)
   and Todoro (1982, pp. 461-464).
2. Later incorporated into the Municipality of Dhaka.
3. See, for examples of this development Muzmanian and
   Sabatier (1983), Sabatier and Muzmanian (1979), Ingram
   and Mann (1980), Nakamura and Smallwood (1980), and
   Palumbo and Harder (1981). Parallel advances have
   been made in the development field, although these
   have primarily been in the area of development administration. See Lindenberg and Crosby (1981), Grant
   (1979) and World Bank (1980, Chapter 6).
4. Davidoff and Reiner (1962, pp. 103-115). For a recent
   survey of the theoretical positions in planning at
   present, see Healey, McDougall and Thomas (1982, pp.
   5-22).
5. An earlier version of some of these ideas was published
   in Choguill (1980).
6. For an overview of the situation in Bangladesh, see
   Pramanik (1982).
7. Further cases are given in Stewart (1978, Chapter 3).
8. See too, Melgolugbe (1983).

References

Aneroussi, F. et al., 1977,   Analysis of Planning and
    Implementation Procedures in Greece (mimeo), Organ-
    ization for Economic Cooperation and Development
    Symposium on the Implementation of Urban Plans,
    CT/URB/620.
Arnstein, S. R., 1969, A Ladder of Citizen Participation,
    Journal of the American Institute of Planners,
    35:216-224.
Ataç, M., 1977, Country Report: Turkey (mimeo), Organ-
    ization for the Economic Cooperation and Development
    Symposium on the Implementation of Urban Plans,
    CT/URB/623.
Barrett, S., and Fudge, C., 1981, "Policy and Action:
    Essays on the Implementation of Public Policy",
    Methuen, London.
Choguill, C. L., 1980, Towards a Theory of Implementation
    in Planning based on the Bangladesh Experience,
    Journal of Administration Overseas, 19:148-159.
Costa Lobo, N. L., 1977, Clandestine Housing Rehabilitation
    - A Continuous Planning and Management Process
    (mimeo), Organization for Economic Cooperation and
    Development Symposium on the Implementation of Urban
    Plans, CT/URB/610.
Dekleva, J., Bon, R., and Music, V. B., 1977, Implemen-
    tation Mechanisms in the System of Social Planning in
    the Context of Socialist Self Management (mimeo),
    Organization for Economic Cooperation and Development
    Symposium on the Implementation of Urban Plans,
    CT/URB/624.
Faludi, A., 1973, "Planning Theory", Pergamon Press,
    Oxford.
Friedmann, J., 1972, Implementation, International Social
    Development Review, 4.
Friedmann, J., 1967, A Conceptual Model for the Analysis of
    Planning Behavior, Administrative Science Quarterly,
    12:225-252.
Grant, G., 1979, "Development Administration: Meaning and
    Application", University of Wisconsin Press, Madison.
Healey, P., McDougall, G., and Thomas, M. J., 1982,
    Theoretical Debates in Planning: Towards a Coherent
    Dialogue, in: "Planning Theory: Prospects for the
    1980s", P. Healey, G. McDougall and M. J. Thomas,
    eds., Pergamon Press, Oxford, pp. 5-22.

Ingram, H. M., and Mann, D., 1980, Why Policies Succeed
    or Fail, Sage Yearbook in Politics and Public Policy, 8,
    Sage, Beverley Hills.
Killick, T., 1976, The Possibilities of Development Planning,
    Oxford Economic Papers, 28.
Lindenberg, M., and Crosby, B., 1981, "Managing Develop-
    ment: The Political Dimension", Kumarion Press, West
    Hartford, Connecticut.
Lipton, M., 1977, "Why Poor People Stay Poor: A Study of
    Urban Bias in World Development", Temple Smith,
    London.
Mazmanian, D. A., and Sabatier, P. A., 1983, "Implemen-
    tation and Public Policy", Scott, Foresman and
    Company, Glenview, Illinois.
Melgolugbe, I. F., 1983, The Hopes and Failures of Public
    Housing in Nigeria, Third World Planning Review,
    5:349-369.
Nakamura, R., and Smallwood, F., 1980, "The Politics of
    Policy Implementation", St. Martins Press, New York.
Nehru, Jawaharlal, 1961, Annual Address by the Prime
    Minister, Indian Journal of Public Administration, 7.
Palumbo, D. J., and Harden, M. A., 1981, "Implementing
    Public Policy", Lexington Books, Lexington,
    Massachusetts.
Pramanik, A. H., 1982, "Development Through Urban Bias
    Public Expenditure: An Empirical Study of Bangladesh",
    University of Dhaka Center for Social Studies, Dhaka.
Pressman, J. L., and Wildavsky, A., 1973, "Implementation:
    How Great Expectations in Washington are Dashed in
    Oakland", University of California Press, Berkeley.
Republic of Nigeria, 1970, "National Development Plan
    1970-1974", Government Printer, Lagos.
Rondinelli, D. A., 1977, "Planning Development Projects",
    Dowden, Hutchinson and Ross, Stroudsburg,
    Pennsylvania.
Sabatier, P. A., and Mazmanian, D. A., 1979, The Con-
    ditions of Effective Implementation: A Guide for
    Accomplishing Policy Objections, Policy Analysis,
    5:481-504.
Stewart, F., 1978, "Technology and Underdevelopment", 2nd
    edition, Macmillan, London.
Todoro, M., 1982, "Economic Development in the Third
    World", 2nd edition, Longman, London.
Van Meter, D. S., and Van Horn, C. E., 1975, The Policy
    Implementation Process: A Conceptual Framework,
    Administration and Society, 6:445-488.

Vepa, R. K., 1974, The Problem of Achieving Results,
    Indian Journal of Public Administration, 20:257-291.
Waterston, A., 1965, "Development Planning: Lessons of
    Experience", The Johns Hopkins Press, Baltimore.
World Bank, 1980, "World Development Report 1980",
    Washington DC.

CHAPTER 2

Footnotes

1. Bangladesh Census Commission (1975). Unfortunately,
   it is known that even the census data are subject to
   error as it is estimated that an under-enumeration of 6%
   occurred in all areas except the major cities of Dhaka,
   Narayanganj, Chittagong and Khulna where the under-
   enumeration was perhaps 16%. The United Nations-
   sponsored National Physical Planning Project in their
   calculations assumed an under-enumeration of 19.3% in
   these four largest metropolitan areas and their estimate
   is used in this study. As a result, in the present
   analysis Dhaka's 1974 population will be assumed to
   have been 2,003,729 rather than the figure 1,679,572 as
   reported by the census. Bangladesh National Physical
   Planning Project/Urban Development Directorate (1979).
2. Certain of these theoretical inconsistencies are
   discussed in Choguill (1983).
3. Administratively, Bangladesh is divided into four
   divisions, twenty-one districts and 71 subdivisions.
   There is a tendency for numbers within these administrative categories to increase over time. Although the
   data used in the analysis refer to the 1961 to 1974
   period, the number of subdivisions which could be used
   totalled 68, the number in existence at the end of 1979.
4. Net cropped areas for rice production in 1975/1976 are
   found in Ministry of Agriculture and Forests (1979,
   Volume I).
5. Consumption of 15 ounces per day is the middle range
   figure used in Robinson (1973, p. 4). Total national
   food grain requirements using consumption rates of 14
   and 16 ounces per day are included. Chen (1975)
   suggests that 14.5 ounces per day could be construed
   as a "reasonably safe level" and that in 1962/1963 the
   consumption dropped to an average of 13.1 ounces.

6. Bangladesh Bureau of Statistics (1976, p. 221).
    Alamgir (1974) provides further evidence along these
    lines when he notes that the ratio of rural to urban
    wages was less than unity for 14 different years
    between 1958 and 1973.
7. A situation which, interestingly, reversed itself after
    1976.
8. For orientation purposes, Old Dhaka is the traditional
    part of the city. The central business district extends
    from there northward to the newer Motijheel Commercial
    Area. Ramna is the "colonial" area, established by the
    British, containing many government buildings and the
    universities. Sher-E-Bangla Nagar contains the new
    capital and government office buildings. Dhanmandi
    and Gulshan are examples of upper middle class resi-
    dential areas. In recent years, Gulshan has become
    increasingly popular with the expatriate community.
9. For a description of such situations, see Shakur (1979)
    and Center for Urban Studies (1979).
10. Using Center for Urban Studies data with an admittedly
    arbitrary sample, Chaudhury, Ahmed and Huda (1976,
    p. 108) suggest that of squatters present in Dhaka in
    1973, 12% had been there since before 1949, 18% moved
    in during the period 1950 to 1960, 52% from 1961 to 1971
    and 18% in 1972 and 1973. The annual rate of growth
    is thus nearly four times higher in 1972-1973 than in
    1961-1971.
11. An interesting comparison can be made with the total
    male population of Bangladesh, where 22% of males were
    within the age group 25-44 and 15% were over 44.
12. Center for Urban Studies (1976, p. 48). In Bangladesh
    as a whole, according to the 1974 Census, the literacy
    rate was 30% for males and 14% for females.
13. Qadir (1975, p. 35). Among specific occupations listed
    were a tailor, a trader of used garments, a mason's
    assistant, a bamboo fence maker, a painter, a flour mill
    worker, a guard, a night mechanic, a taxi driver, a
    signboard maker, a motor mechanic, one who bought
    wheat from ration drawers and then resold it, a sub-
    contractor, a grave digger, a shoe factory worker, a
    vegetable vendor, a carpenter, a pushcart driver, a
    cook, a gardener, a member of the river police and a
    private tutor.
14. The CUS identified 119 clusters of squatters within the
    Dhaka area.

References

Alamgir, M., 1974, Some Analysis of Distribution of Income,
    Consumption, Saving and Poverty in Bangladesh, The
    Bangladesh Development Studies, 2:737-818.
Alim, A., 1974, "An Introduction to Bangladesh Agricul-
    ture", Swadesh Printing Press, Dhaka.
Bangladesh Bureau of Statistics, 1985, "Statistical Yearbook
    of Bangladesh 1983-1984", Dhaka.
Bangladesh Bureau of Statistics, 1983, "1982 Statistical
    Yearbook of Bangladesh", Dhaka.
Bangladesh Bureau of Statistics, 1979, "1979 Statistical
    Yearbook of Bangladesh", Dhaka.
Bangladesh Bureau of Statistics, 1976, "Statistical Yearbook
    of Bangladesh 1975", Dhaka.
Bangladesh Census Commission, 1975, "Bangladesh Census of
    Population 1974", Dhaka.
Bangladesh National Physical Planning Project/Urban Devel-
    opment Directorate, 1979, "Selected Background Infor-
    mation on Population and Urbanization in Bangladesh",
    Working Paper Number 1.
Center for Urban Studies, 1979, University of Dhaka, "The
    Urban Poor in Bangladesh", a research report of
    UNICEF, Dhaka.
Center for Urban Studies, 1976, University of Dhaka,
    "Squatters in Bangladesh Cities", Dhaka.
Chaudhury, R. H., Ahmed, N. R., and Huda, S., 1976,
    Management of Immigrants to Urban Regions of
    Bangladesh, in: "National Report on Human Settlements:
    Bangladesh", Government of the People's Republic of
    Bangladesh, Prepared for the Habitat Conference,
    Vancouver, pp. 85-114.
Chen, L. C., 1975, An Analysis of Per Capita Food Grain
    Availability, Consumption and Requirements in
    Bangladesh: A Systematic Approach to Food Planning,
    The Bangladesh Development Studies, 3:93-126.
Chen, L. C., and Rohde, J. E., 1973, Civil War in
    Bangladesh: Famine Averted?, in: "Disaster in
    Bangladesh", L. C. Chen, ed., Oxford University
    Press, New York.
Choguill, C. L., 1983, Migration and its Implications for
    Urban Development, Regional Development Dialogue,
    4:66-81.
Faaland, J., and Parkinson, J. R., 1976, "Bangladesh: Test
    Case for Development", University Press, Dhaka.

Government of the People's Republic of Bangladesh, 1975,
    National Report: Bangladesh, Prepared for the Habitat
    Regional Conference in Tehran, Dhaka.
Jahan, R., 1974, Bangladesh in 1973: Management of
    Factional Politics, Asian Survey, 14:125-135.
Johnson, B. L. C., 1975, "Bangladesh", Heinemann,
    London.
Kahn, A. M. M., Amanat Ullah, 1975/1976, Land Value
    Pattern in Dacca, Oriental Geographer, 19/20.
Khan, M. S. A., and Alam, M. K., 1973, "Facts about
    Squatters, Dacca City" (mimeo).
Ministry of Agriculture and Forests, 1979, Agro-Economic
    Research, "Thana Level Agriculture of Bangladesh
    1975-1976", Dhaka.
Ministry of Public Works, 1975, Eviction and Temporary
    Rehabilitation of Squatters at Dattapara, Demra and
    Mirpur (Phase I), Dacca (mimeo).
Muhammad, N., 1974, "Some Aspects of Bangladesh Demo-
    graphic Survey" (mimeo).
Planning Commission, 1980, The Second Five Year Plan
    1980-1985, Dhaka.
Qadir, S. R., 1975, "Bastees of Dacca: A Study of Squatter
    Settlement", Local Government Institute, Dhaka.
Robinson, A., 1973, "Economic Prospects of Bangladesh",
    Overseas Development Institute, London.
Shakur, M. T., 1979, "Physical Upgrading of a Low Income
    Community in Dacca", Unpublished Joint Master's
    Degree Thesis in Urban and Regional Planning,
    Bangladesh University of Engineering and Technology/
    University of Sheffield.
Stepanek, J. F., 1979, "Bangladesh - Equitable Growth?",
    Pergamon Press, New York.
Sommer, A., and Mosley, W. H., 1973, The Cyclone: Medical
    Assessment and Determination of Relief and Rehabili-
    tation Requirements, in: "Disaster in Bangladesh", L.
    C. Chen, ed., Oxford University Press, New York.
The Guardian, 1974, 13 August.
World Bank, 1983, "World Bank Atlas", Washington DC.
World Bank, 1979, "Bangladesh: Current Trends and Devel-
    opment Issues", Washington DC.

CHAPTER 3

Footnotes

1. For an insider's view of the background leading to the Plan, see Islam (1977).
2. For a fuller description of the urban planning system of Bangladesh, see Choguill (1984). Much of the present description is extracted from that source and is reproduced with the permission of the publisher.
3. The East Bengal Building Construction Act, 1952 (East Bengal Act II of 1952).
4. The Town Improvement Act, 1953 (East Bengal Act XIII of 1953).
5. Like much of Bangladesh planning legislation, the "improvement trust" can be traced to British antecedents, although this time in an indirect manner. The East Bengal Town Improvement Act of 1953 is modeled very closely on the Calcutta Improvement Act of 1911 which in turn seems to be based on the Glasgow Improvement Trust of 1866.
6. Town Improvement (Amendment) Ordinances, 1958, Sections 73-75.
7. A fourth was added for Rajshahi in 1976 but this is, of course, after the period of our present investigation. Planning in other urban areas is allowed under other legislation passed or amended since the end of this period as well, particularly under the terms of the Paurashava Ordinance of 1977 which was designed to "provide for the constitution of local government institutions in urban areas and to consolidate and amend certain laws relating to local government in such areas".
8. United Nations (1973). The mission consisted of Dr P. S. Towfighi, Team leader, Mr R. Mora-Rubio of the UN Center for Housing Building and Planning, and Mr H. Boldrick of the International Cooperative Housing Development Association.
9. The first of these estimates was based on the Mission's own survey of the squatter situation in Dhaka, published by Khan and Alam (1973). The second and third were by Hussain (1973) and Department of Geography, Dhaka University (1973).

References

Abedin, Z., 1970, Impact of Rapid Development of Cities and Towns in East Pakistan on Law Enforcement Agency, in: "Our Cities and Towns", M. J. Abedin, ed., National Institute of Public Administration, Dhaka.

Alam, M. K., 1979, "Proposal for an Integrated Development Planning Organization for the Dacca Metropolitan Area", Unpublished Joint Master's Degree Thesis in Urban and Regional Planning, Bangladesh University of Engineering and Technology/University of Sheffield.

Alam, S., 1970, Maintenance of Beautifying Cities and Towns, in: "Our Cities and Towns", M. J. Abedin, ed., National Institute of Public Administration, Dhaka.

Anisuzzaman, M., 1979, "Bangladesh Public Administration and Society", Bangladesh Books International, Dhaka.

Bangladesh Bureau of Statistics, 1979, "1979 Statistical Yearbook of Bangladesh", Dhaka.

Choguill, C. L., 1984, Dacca: An Analysis of Planning Implementation, Past and Future, in: "Urban Innovation Abroad: Problem Cities in Search of Solutions", T. L. Blair, ed., Plenum Press, New York, pp. 138-157.

Dainik Bangla, 1974, 25 March.

Dainik Bangla, 1973, 17 August.

Department of Geography, Dhaka University, 1973, "Bulletin of Center for Urban Studies", 4, November.

Gerull, B., 1979, "Economic Effects of Housing in Developing Countries, Vol. III: Field Study in Bangladesh, Part A: Analysis of Two Types of Low-Income Residential Areas in Dacca", Institute of Tropical Building and Planning, University of Darmstadt, Darmstadt.

Government of East Pakistan, 1965, Water, Power and Irrigation Department, "Government Order No. 464-E", 17 July, Dhaka.

Hafiz, M. A., 1979, Physical Layout of Our Cities and Towns as it Relates to Greater Khulna, in: "Our Cities and Towns", M. J. Abedin, ed., National Institute of Public Administration, Dhaka.

Hussain, A. Z. M. W., 1973, "Squatting and Squatters in Dacca City: 1972", Unpublished Master of Arts Thesis, Department of Geography, University of Dhaka.

Islam, N., 1978, "Development Strategy of Bangladesh", Pergamon Press, Oxford.

Islam, N., 1977, "Development Planning in Bangladesh", Hurst, London.

James, J. R., 1973, A Discussion Paper on Some Aspects of
    Town and Country Planning in Bangladesh, The Ford
    Foundation (mimeo), Dhaka.
Khan, M. S. A., and Alam, M. K., 1973, Facts about
    Squatters - Dacca City, Urban Development Directorate,
    Ministry of Public Works and Urban Development
    (mimeo), Dhaka.
Minoprio, Spenceley and P. W. Macfarlane, 1959, "Master
    Plan for Dacca", London.
Noman, A., 1970, Anti-Social Activities, in: "Our Cities and
    Towns", M. J. Abedin, ed., National Institute of Public
    Administration, Dhaka.
Pakistan Planning Commission, 1968, "Third Five Year Plan",
    abridged edition, Karachi.
Pakistan Planning Commission, 1960, "Second Five Year Plan
    1960-1965", Karachi.
Planning Commission, 1978, "The Two Year Plan 1978-1980",
    Dhaka.
Planning Commission, 1974, "Economic Development in 1973-
    1974 and Annual Plan for 1974-1975", Dhaka.
Planning Commission, 1973, "The First Five Year Plan
    1973-1978", Dhaka.
Rahman, G., 1970, Metropolitan Administration: Planning and
    Development Aspects, in: "Our Cities and Towns", M.
    J. Abedin, ed., National Institute of Public Admin-
    istration, Dhaka.
Robinson, A., 1973, "Economic Prospects of Bangladesh",
    Overseas Development Institute, London.
Sher, O. S., 1979, "Profile of Mirpur: Profiles of Three
    Developing Areas within the Dacca Metropolitan Area",
    United Nations Development Program/Bangladesh Urban
    Development Directorate, Dhaka.
United Nations, 1973, "Mission on Urban Squatters", Project
    of the Government of the People's Republic of
    Bangladesh, BGD/73/017, November-December.
Urban Development Directorate, 1968, Genesis of Physical
    Planning in East Pakistan, "Physical Planning
    Progress", Dhaka.
Zaman, M. A., 1973, "Background Paper: Possible UNDP
    Assistance to Housing in Bangladesh", Prepared in
    conjunction with A. C. Das and M. A. Zaman, Draft
    memorandum to the Minister of Public Works and Urban
    Development, 23 January.

CHAPTER 4

Footnotes

1. These latter two points were originally a part of the
    so-called "11-Point Program" that was drawn up in 1968
    by the East Bengal Students Action Committee which
    unified what had previously been disparate policies of
    the Awami League and the left-wing student organ-
    izations, particularly the Student Union, linked to the
    Moscow-oriented National Awami League.
2. It is interesting to note that, according to data tabu-
    lated by Chaudhuri (1969, pp. 134-135), privilege was
    almost a prerequisite for entry into the Pakistani Civil
    Service in the mid-1960s. In 1963 and 1964, of the 677
    candidates for civil service positions whose fathers had
    an annual income of less than 1,000 rupees per year,
    only 15% were successful. Of the 72 candidates whose
    fathers earned over 32,000 rupees, 32% were successful.
    In a nation that was composed predominantly of
    farmers, over 31% of the civil service entrants in 1964
    were sons of businessmen, teachers, lawyers and
    engineers.
3. The Deputy Chairman of the Planning Commission (the
    Head of State was titular Chairman) was Professor
    Nurul Islam, while the members were Professors Anisur
    Rahman, Mosharraf Hussain and Rahman Sobban.
4. Interview with Moinrul Islam, Permanent Secretary at
    the Ministry of Public Works and Urban Development at
    that time, 14 May 1980.
5. Jinzara, for example, has repeatedly been mentioned as
    the possible site of a satellite "new town", including the
    community and the rest of Keraniganj Island. See
    Ministry of Public Works and Urban Development (1978).
6. No. 1982-JS (UD). Among the eleven points included
    in this order were that unauthorized construction in
    certain parts of the city should be demolished, that
    certain abandoned houses occupied by private organ-
    izations should be cleared, that overdue rents on shops
    and markets should be collected within two weeks of the
    order and, perhaps ironically under the grave circum-
    stances, that the possibility of construction of further
    three and four room housing units for government
    officers should be explored.
7. Translated by T. A. Khan, in Khan (1979, p. 42).

8. Interview with Moinrul Islam, who in addition to being
    Permanent Secretary at the Ministry of Public Works
    and Urban Development, had been appointed Chairman
    of the Resettlement Planning Committee, 14 May 1980.

References

Anisuzzaman, M., 1979, "Bangladesh Public Administration
    and Society", Bangladesh Books International, Dhaka.
Bangladesh Times, 1975a, 4 January.
Bangladesh Times, 1975b, 10 January.
Bangladesh Times, 1975c, 17 January.
Bangladesh Times, 1982, 29 May.
Campbell, D. (1981), Bangladesh and the Landless, Paper
    presented at the Development Studies Association
    Annual Meeting, Oxford University.
Chaudhury, R. H., Ahmed, N. R., and Huda, S., 1976,
    Management of Immigrants to Urban Regions of
    Bangladesh, in: "National Report on Human Settlements:
    Bangladesh", Government of the People's Republic of
    Bangladesh, Prepared for the UN Conference on Human
    Settlements in Vancouver, p. 114.
Islam, N., 1977, "Development Planning in Bangladesh",
    Hurst, London.
Khan, T. A., 1979, "A Study of the Process of Integration
    of Squatter Settlements in Greater Dacca", Unpublished
    Joint Master's Degree Thesis in Urban and Regional
    Planning, Bangladesh University of Engineering and
    Technology/University of Sheffield.
Ministry of Public Works and Urban Development, 1978,
    "Establishment of a New City at Keraniganj", Dhaka.
Ministry of Public Works and Urban Development, 1979,
    "Eviction and Temporary Rehabilitation of Squatters at
    Dattapara, Demra and Mirpur (Phase I)", Dhaka.
Shakur, M. T., 1985, Changing Attitude of the "Concerned
    Groups" Toward Squatter Settlements in Dhaka,
    Bangladesh: A Case Study, Paper presented at
    Symposium on Change within the Built Environment,
    Oxford Polytechnic, 21-22 February.
The Guardian, 1975, 18 February.
The Guardian, 1976, 2 January.

CHAPTER 5

Footnotes

1. Which as a result of a reorganization in 1979 was absorbed into the new United Nations Center for Human Settlements (HABITAT) and was transferred from New York to Nairobi.
2. These points are extracted from a memorandum from F. H. Abed, on behalf of the Bangladesh Rural Advancement Committee, to OXFAM's Dhaka office, in reply to questions with respect to a prospective interest-free loan from OXFAM to BRAC, dated 27 September 1978.
3. Draft Grant Agreement, "Mirpur Resettlement Program", March 1978, Annex 1.

References

Campbell, D., 1981, "Bangladesh and the Landless", Paper presented at the Development Studies Association Annual Meeting, Oxford University, September.

Finucane, A., 1978, "Statement on CONCERN's Interest in Bashantek", 25 July.

OXFAM, 1978, "OXFAM Project: BD55 Feeding, Housing and Sanitation Programs in Demra and Bashantek Bustee Camps, Dacca", March.

United Nations Capital Development Fund (UNCDF, 1977), "Mirpur Squatters Resettlement Project", Report of Mission to the People's Republic of Bangladesh, March 1977, prepared by G. Gabella, dated July.

United Nations Capital Development Fund (UNCDF, 1978), "Mirpur Squatters Resettlement Project", Report of Mission to the People's Republic of Bangladesh, September 1977 - January 1978, prepared by D. Etherton and A. C. Lewin, 27 January.

CHAPTER 6

Footnotes

1. As there were very few agricultural workers in the sample, it is assumed that no seasonal variation exists.
2. Gross National Product estimates for the period 1974 to 1978 are found in World Bank (1979).

3. This is, of course, based on a number of very strong
   assumptions such as the acceptability in the longer term
   of the differential rent system, the continued goodwill
   of the Government in providing interest-free credit, no
   housing or settlement maintenance charges for the
   inhabitants, a continuation of this rather high rate of
   growth and no change in the marginal propensities to
   consume as incomes increase. In effect, this set of
   assumptions gives the most favorable financial picture
   possible.

References

Ahmeduzzaman, M., 1979, "The Rising Cost of Urban Land:
    A Report on the Land Market in Savar, Bangladesh",
    Unpublished Joint Master's Degree Thesis in Urban and
    Regional Planning, Bangladesh University of Engineer-
    ing and Technology/University of Sheffield.
Khan, M. D. A., and Alam, M. K., 1973, Facts about
    Squatters: Dacca City, Bangladesh Urban Development
    Directorate (mimeo).
Ministry of Public Works and Urban Development, 1975a,
    "Rough Estimate for Eviction of Squatters Unauthor-
    izedly Occupying Land of Government and other
    Agencies and their Temporary Rehabilitation at
    Dattapara, Demra and Mirpur Including Removal of
    Unauthorized Markets and Recovery of Possession of
    Government Properties: General Abstract", Dhaka.
Ministry of Public Works and Urban Development, 1975b,
    "Rough Estimate for Resettlement of Urban Squatters at
    Dacca, Mirpur", Dhaka.
Prakash, V., 1985, Affordability and Cost Recovery of
    Urban Services for the Poor, Regional Development
    Dialogue, 6:1-39.
United Nations, 1973, "Mission on Urban Squatters", Project
    of the Government of the People's Republic of
    Bangladesh, BGD/73/017, November-December.
United Nations Capital Development Fund (UNCDF, 1978),
    "Mirpur Squatters Resettlement Project", Report of
    Mission to the People's Republic of Bangladesh,
    September 1977 - January 1978, prepared by D.
    Etherton and A. C. Lewin, dated 27 January.
United Nations Capital Development Fund (UNCDF, 1977),
    "Mirpur Squatter Resettlement Project", Report of

Mission to the People's Republic of Bangladesh, March
1977, prepared by G. Gabella, dated July 1977.
World Bank, 1979, "Bangladesh: Current Trends and Development Issues, A World Bank Country Study",
Washington DC.

CHAPTER 7

Footnotes

1. Portions of this chapter have appeared in slightly
   different forms in Choguill (1982a) and Choguill (1982b)
   and are used here with permission of the publishers.
2. Site visit memorandum by D. Etherton, 13 June 1979.
3. Coordinating Committee Minutes, 17 June 1978.
4. The issue was discussed at some length by the Coordinating Committee during at least seven meetings
   between 7 July and 21 November 1978.
5. Informal memorandum of BRAC's position with respect to
   the sanitary system, prepared by A. Jenkins,
   presented to the Committee on 15 November 1978.
6. Coordinating Committee Minutes, 20 November 1978.
7. M. R. Haq, President of the Bangladesh Thikador
   Society at the Inaugural Ceremony of the First National
   Convention, 27 May 1973, quoted in World Bank (1978,
   p. 6).
8. Between 13 June 1978 and 25 April 1979, a total of 21
   inspection reports were issued covering approximately
   52 site visits. Personnel involved included representatives of UNDP, UNCDF, OXFAM, CONCERN, BRAC,
   the Bangladesh Water Development Board (including a
   representative of the Netherlands Technical Assistance
   Program who was seconded to this organization and who
   played a leading role in attempting to save the embankment) and HSD. These reports provide the information
   used in analyzing the responsiveness of implementing
   bodies to problems that arose in the course of constructing the embankment.

References

Choguill, C. L., 1982a, Linking Planning and Implementation: The Mirpur Resettlement Project, Ekistics, 49
January/February:37-42.

Choguill, C. L., 1982b, Mirpur Revisited: An Analysis of a
    Squatter Resettlement Scheme, Planning and Develop-
    ment in Developing Countries, Proceedings of PTRC
    Summer Annual Meeting, University of Warwick.
Khan, T. A., 1979, "A Study of the Process of Integration
    of Squatter Settlements in Greater Dacca", Unpublished
    Joint Master's Degree Thesis in Urban and Regional
    Planning, Bangladesh University of Engineering and
    Technology/University of Sheffield.
United Nations Capital Development Fund (UNCDF, 1978),
    "Mirpur Squatters Resettlement Project", Report of a
    Mission to the People's Republic of Bangladesh,
    prepared by D. Etherton and A. C. Lewin, dated 27
    January.
World Bank, 1978, "Bangladesh: Review of Construction
    Industry, December 1977", Report of a Mission to the
    People's Republic of Bangladesh, prepared by H. S.
    Kaden, B. Coukis and J. Henley, Washington DC.

Index

Mirpur squatter resettlement
(continued)
differential rent system,
140-143
Embankment, see
Embankment
estimating costs, 131-133
five different plans,
131-132
finance, 110-111
finances, timing of
availability, 178-179
recovery of costs,
179-180
financial feasibility,
130-151
flood-free site,
comparison studies,
145-149
flat rate system, 143
flooding problems, 108-109
formulating the scheme,
106-111
housing units, 109-110
implementation, 152-174
(see also Implementation)
non-government organ-
izations, 124-125
permanent solution,
102-129
planning stage, 111-117
community buildings, 114
embankment, 111-114
evaluating, 121-125
fresh water supplies, 116
housing, 114
open space/recreation
areas, 114-116
sanitation, 116-117
storm damage, 117
suggested layout,
(Figure) 115
project document, 125-128
recovering costs, 135-136
rent charges, 135

Mirpur squatter resettlement
(continued)
selling to settlers, costs,
136, 137
'ability to pay', 137-139
site, 76, 78
choice and cultural
understanding, 181
costings for preliminary
plans, 80-83
non-government organ-
izations, (Table)
96-98
selection, feasibility of
low/high ground,
145-149
total community repay-
ments, 139-140
United Nations Capital
Development Fund,
107-111
commitment, 117-121
(see also Resettlement,
squatters)
Monetary resources, lack,
and implementation
constraints, 9

Natural disasters,
Bangladesh, 24-27
'Negative powers', 7
Non-government organ-
izations at Tongi,
Demra and Mirpur,
93-100
at Bashantek, early days,
104-105
at Mirpur, 124-125

Occupations of squatters,
Dhaka, 42-44
OXFAM
role in implementation of
Mirpur project, 157
role in resettlement of
squatters, 92-94